E. 'G. Solomon

*How I see America from within
after a 15 year sojourn*

▪ the ▪
Diaries
of an ▪
Immigrant

The Diaries of an Immigrant, by E. 'G. Solomon
Copyright © 2014 by E. 'G. Solomon

ISBN 978-1-60924-046-2

E. 'G. Solomon
1148 Pulaski Highway
Suite 456
Bear, DE 19701

E-mail: egsolomon@diariesofanimmigrant.com

www.DiariesOfAnImmigrant.com

DEDICATION

*I dedicate this book to the millions of people
who have dreamed the American dream,
and have done something about it.*

Nothing will be impossible for you.

- E. 'G. Solomon

Contents

American National Anthem

The Star-Spangled Banner

Oh, say can you see by the dawn's early light

What so proudly we hailed at the twilight's last gleaming?

Whose broad stripes and bright stars thru the perilous fight,

O'er the ramparts we watched were so gallantly streaming?

And the rocket's red glare, the bombs bursting in air,

Gave proof through the night that our flag was still there.

Oh, say does that star-spangled banner yet wave

O'er the land of the free and the home of the brave?

America the Beautiful

O beautiful for spacious skies,

For amber waves of grain,

For purple mountain majesties

Above the fruited plain!

America! America!

God shed His grace on thee,

And crown thy good with brotherhood

From sea to shining sea!

God Bless America

God bless America,

Land that I love,

Stand beside her and guide her

Through the night with a light from above;

From the mountains, to the prairies,

To the oceans white with foam,

God bless America, My home, sweet home.

God bless America, My home, sweet home.

Preface

This book has been written to chronicle some of my observations and experiences from the time my family and I came to live in the United States of America. It has afforded me the opportunity to add my own personal impressions about some of the issues discussed in this book.

America is a vast and complex country. When it is snowing in some part, the temperature could be very high in other parts. If flood is ravaging in one area due to excess rainfall, fire due to drought could be burning acres of land in another.

Every author writing about America life writes from their own perspective. No one book can capture all that America is. No one book like this can completely document the vastness of the land, and the diversity of the peoples and cultures of America. And when describing life in America, you can only describe it from your own knowledge and experience.

I hope that this book will be a source of enlightenment for the peoples of the United States by providing an insight into the thinking of the immigrant population. I also hope that it will become a catalyst for discussing and implementing ideas that may help address some of the issues raised therein, particularly on issues of race, policing, and politics. If serious discussions and new thinking emerge on these issues, a lot would have been achieved.

I am aware that not everyone will agree with some of the viewpoints that I have expressed. Those who don't agree are entitled to their own opinions, as I am entitled to mine.

If this book is able to challenge people to a higher purpose, I am sure that America will be the better for it.

I am grateful to God for giving me the idea and the opportunity to write this book. I am also thankful to the beautiful family God has given me, my lovely wife and my three wonderful children. They help me make meaning out of life.

I am thankful to God for my recruiter Jill Coogan, and other great people God brought my way.

In God We Trust.

E. 'G Solomon
Delaware, USA

Chapter 1

Introduction

When we arrived Philadelphia in
late 1998... there was no Twitter and
no tweets, no Instagram, no Google, and
Facebook would have been something
you borrowed from the library to cover
your visage with.

1
Introduction

I came to the United States in October 1998 to start an IT consulting job with a leading software company. On a prior visit, I was blessed to have been recruited to join a Y2K remediation team that was working to fix old computer software for their clients. The prevailing fear in corporate America at that time was that computer systems running the existing code might crash as the clock turned to usher in the year 2000, leading to a meltdown of computerized services with various probable scenarios of disaster.

America loves to attract talent. They recruit and seek out people with special expertise in their fields from all over the world, especially if there is a shortage of Americans with skills in those fields. Most employers don't care where you come from, as long as you have the skills they need. Because of this, there is a strong and virile population of talents from different parts of the world living and working in America. Such talents have doubtlessly contributed to the growth of knowledge in technology, medicine, and industry in America.

As an immigrant, how fast you settle into the American society depends on how you came in and whom you stay with upon arrival.

Apart from your entry visa, two documents are basic to your stay in America – your social security number (or SSN) and your driver's license. So the first thing you apply for is your SSN. Your SSN is a number without which "no one may buy or sell," as it were, in America. It is the number that uniquely identifies you in the system. When you get it, you can apply for a driver's license or anything else you need.

In pre-9/11 days, you could get an SSN, even as a visitor. I got mine when I needed to open a bank account in New York on a visit in the early 90s. As a visitor, you would get one that stipulates "NOT VALID FOR EMPLOYMENT." When your employment status changes and you get a work authorization or work visa, all you have to do is reapply for a new card. While the new card will not bear the restriction the visitor card has, it will still show the same number - you always retain your number even when your status changes. But things have changed in America. Today, even as a bona-fide foreign student, you cannot get an SSN. As a foreigner, you now need a work authorization to get an SSN.

As for how you came in, it depends on if you came in legally, with a green card or work visa, or if you came in with a non-immigrant visitor's visa, and you want to work your way to staying in the system.

Some people came in with a visitor's visa that does not allow them to work. The problem today is that someone with a visitor's visa who is trying to settle can hardly breathe in the current immigration regime. They cannot get an SSN. Even if they got an SSN, the US Citizenship and Immigration Service (USCIS) now makes employers sign on to a system called E-Verify in order to determine the employment eligibility of any prospective worker – so they cannot get any regular work.

The same situation applies to those who come in across the border without any visa at all. For those who came in many years ago when the laws were more relaxed, they are now an integral part of the United States more or less as they must have overcome these hurdles over the years.

Things are much harder for those coming into the system now. Everywhere seems to be blocked. Short of doing odd jobs (of which there aren't many) and receiving under-the-table wages, there doesn't seem to be a way to live today in America as a new undocumented immigrant.

In my own case, I came in with an H1B work visa. This visa entitled me to stay and work and allowed me to bring in my family as well. Therefore, I had no down time on arrival, as I had to report for work just 2 days later. Six weeks later, I rented an apartment and my family arrived. We were truly blessed to have things work for us the way they did.

Coming into the US with a job waiting for you is the best situation a person can get. It helps you integrate into the American society fast and be less dependent on your hosts.

How easily you integrate into the system depends on where you arrived at, and whom you stay with on arrival. There are people who came in on even an immigrant visa or green card, but had to wait for days or weeks before getting their basic documents. Since they don't know their way around, they have to depend on others to help them as they try to obtain these documents.

With the importance of your SSN, you can imagine if, on your arrival, your hosts are so busy that for the first four weeks, they have no time to get you to the Social Security Administration office to apply for your SSN. This means, for those first few weeks, you are in limbo, watching American TV while the people you left back in your country are thinking that you had settled in and were doing fine. I have seen someone who couldn't get to the Driver's License office for 6 months – because their host was busy!

Some Things I Have Learned

Despite the fact that I came into America when I was of age, I have, nevertheless, learned many new things. Some of these were due to the fact that I had studied in Nigeria, a former British colony, where we were taught Queen's English.

I have learned that "labour" has to be "labor," and "honour" is now "honor." When a car overtakes another on the road, what it actually did was "pass" that car. A "roundabout" becomes a turning circle, and instead of forming a "queue," you form a line. You don't write a "cheque," but you can write a check, and you don't go to the "toilet" but to the bathroom. Looking back, I wonder why the British couldn't keep it simple – spell it as you call it - as it is done in America. The British spellings are like taking the most difficult questions on a test just to show you are brilliant!

I have learned that the football I grew up with should be called "soccer," and a sport where we carry a "ball" with our hands while wearing helmets should be called "football." The "ball" is not even round, as most game balls are, but oblong, unlike the round balls in tennis, ping pong, soccer, basketball, volleyball, squash, golf, cricket, and almost every other game.

I have learned that a Senator elected to Congress is not a Congressman, but a Senator, while, at the same time, a Congressman is someone elected to Congress. You never call a Senator a Congressman, yet he is a member of Congress.

There is no school set up to orientate immigrants on these and many other changes, you just sort of pick it up – something like "What They Didn't Teach You In Whatever-School-You-Went-To-Wherever-You-Are-Coming-From" kind of thing. Your first guide is your word processing software – Microsoft Word for example, as it underlines in red the words you have to change, indicating they are spelling errors, including your name. Then you realize, oh, I'm in America!

No one knows tomorrow

The times have surely changed, and if you look at life in America today compared to when I arrived, I would seem like a dinosaur.

When we arrived Philadelphia in late 1998, there was no GPS system in common use, so we travelled using Rand McNally map books. There was no Twitter and no tweets, no Instagram, no Google, and Facebook would have been something you borrowed from the library to cover your visage with. No one went around carrying tiny computer devices into which telephone-on-the-go functionality had been built. Today they call them cell phones, but the "phone" function is just one of the many uses of these devices.

Most people, I would guess 90% of Americans, didn't have cell phones. We made calls from our home phones which are now known as land lines. If you were away from home, there were AT&T and Bell-Atlantic phone booths in many places and around most street corners. You made calls by dropping in quarter coins, and if you had no quarter and couldn't beg for one from people passing, you could make collect calls. A collect call is one where you call an operator at an easy-to-remember number, and the operator would then call the number you give them and ask the other party if they were willing to accept charges for the call. Only when they agree to accept the charges would your call be connected. This assumes you knew the number of the person you wanted to call. Yes, we knew people's telephone numbers – either from memory, or from some little phone-book or diary you carried everywhere. Those days are gone, but it was just yesterday!

Today, nobody knows any other person's number off the top of their heads. The little computers, sorry, cell phones we carry around, have spoilt us. Why bother, when you can select by name, or command the phone - or your car - "call Muyi," and it does so. And when your spouse or friend calls you, their photograph appears as the phone rings. You can even make the phone ring differently if it's a close friend, or ring with another tone for people you don't want to talk to. To say that all these changes happened in so few years is almost unbelievable.

We took photographs by loading into a camera a 24 or 36-exposure film you bought from Rite-Aid or some other store and snap your pictures over several days or weeks (or months) until all the exposures were used up. You would then rewind the film and take it back to Rite-Aid or any other pho-to handling store, where you would pay for the development and printing of the pictures. It was only when the photos had been developed and printed that you could actually see what ANY of the pictures you had taken looked like. America didn't have the ability to take a picture and instantly review it to decide if a retake was necessary. The closest to that was the Polaroid cameras, which developed and produced pictures instantly, but you still had to use up a film exposure.

No one searched you before you entered a plane. You could go anywhere you liked in an airport and there were airports where you could go and watch the planes take off. The pilot flying an aircraft could invite passengers into the cockpit. If a pilot tried that today, the Department of Homeland Security would be waiting for him as the plane landed. And before they carted him away, they would allow the airline to hand him a letter of termination of his appointment.

In the historic age when I came into America, 15 long years ago, the name synonymous with being stupendously rich was Rockefeller or Gates, and certainly not Buffett, nor Koch. At that time, most politicians would have dismissed the idea of a not-so-bright scion of the first President Bush becoming a future President of the United States, not to mention of him becoming a later statesman. No one knew that the towering Speaker of the House of Representatives Newt Gingrich would become available for a TV show, basking in the old glory of his encounters of the 1990s with President Bill Clinton. You couldn't have guessed that Tom Delay would be delayed from political glory.

If anyone had predicted, right after the Monica Lewinsky scandal, that there would be an organization called the Clinton Global Initiative, people would have thought it would be for some salacious knowledge the beloved President wanted to pass to current Presidents all over the world of how to do some kind of stuff while seated at the Presidential office table, and not a giant world-class development-oriented organization it is today. Certainly, no one predicted the resurrection and the second rising of Bill Clinton, or that America would develop a serious hunger for his wife, Hillary Clinton, to be introduced as "the next President of the United States" at campaign rallies.

No one could have predicted that a day would ever come when nineteen young men, under the cloak of coming to America for education and visit, would band together and execute a terrorist strike against America from within. Even the CIA analysts who were convinced that a terrorist strike against America was imminent could not say what the nature, the place, or the time of the expected enemy action would be. On September 11, 2001, everyone was caught off-guard. Nineteen. That's too big a number to avoid detection by all of the multi-layered law-enforcement organizations in this country, even back in 2001. Thank God, things have changed and are more coordinated now. And no one knew it would take more than ten years for the terrorists' sponsor, Osama bin Laden, to be discovered and killed.

No one in their right senses could have predicted that an American-born Kenyan-American would, within ten years from the day of my arrival in the US, be elected President of the United States of America. No one could have predicted that a couple of months after, he would be crowned by Newsweek magazine as the most influential person on earth, and receive a Nobel Prize for Peace.

No one knew that a bare-armed black lawyer would become the First Lady of the United States and live in the White House with her black husband, her black children and her black mother!

As it is said in Africa, no one knows tomorrow.

Chapter 2

Witness to History

Everything was relaxed then, and
you wouldn't even imagine that anyone would think of bringing dangerous
objects onboard a plane to harm other
passengers. But on 9/11, that world lost
its innocence.

2
Witness to History

I have lived in America for 15 years, but if you look at the sheer quantum of events that happened in this span of time, it seems to have been a life time.

September 11, 2001

I was living in America on September 11, 2001 or 9/11, the day the America we knew changed forever. It was so much like a bad movie that very few movies have been made about it, even thirteen years later. On that day, more than 3,000 Americans were killed, as passenger planes hijacked by terrorists rammed into the twin towers of the World Trade Center, the Pentagon, and a field in Pennsylvania. The attack against America was not just audacious, but vicious and evil. Those who planned it and those who executed it were very mean-hearted and wicked, not considering that the passengers on those planes and those killed on the ground were some other people's fathers and mothers, sons and daughters, brothers and sisters, nephews, nieces, and cousins.

The wickedness inflicted on America, the humiliation of the country – yes it was deep humiliation - and the taking of so many innocent lives in cold blood in a non-battle situation makes 9/11 go down into eternal infamy. Many still do not believe that the USA finding and killing the motivator of that attack, Osama bin Laden 10 years later, was sufficient to atone for that tragedy. For all the changes that had to be introduced into civil aviation and everyday living, locking up a few bad guys does not seem to be enough.

Before 9/11, when friends you had not seen in a while had a stop-over at the Philadelphia International Airport, you would go to the airport and visit with them at the gate while they waited for their connecting flights. Everything was relaxed then, and you wouldn't even imagine that anyone would think of bringing dangerous objects onboard a plane to harm other passengers. But on 9/11, that world lost its innocence.

The security regime at the airports is now so institutionalized that younger people might not even know that there was a time when those security structures were not there. I think there is so much more evil in this world today than there has ever been at any other time in history. Killing off whole neighborhoods of human beings does not move people's consciences. The sad thing about it is that these killings happen today not just in one place, but in several parts of the world, at the same time.

Y2K

I was in Philadelphia at the turn of the millennium. In fact, the employment that had brought me to the US was to join one of the teams that fanned out across the land to help governments and businesses remediate their legacy computer software in readiness for Y2K. Alas, the year 2000 came and went, and the world was still standing. It is not that the doomsday scenarios were fabricated. There could have been some systems failures if there were no remediation efforts, but no one could accurately forecast then, and now, what systems would have failed and which ones would have stood. Well, thank God for the panic created, it brought people like me to the US on the basis of our skills.

Monica!

I was in America during the Monica Lewinsky case, and President Bill Clinton's impeachment trials. The events were like a movie. Republicans in their 50s and 60s spirited away a 22 year old intern, young enough to be younger than the youngest daughter of most of them, and barraged her with questions, threatening her with perjury. Although I had no skin in the game, and while I thought President Clinton messed up badly and was reckless (something I believe he regrets till this day), I nevertheless came to the conclusion that those Republican leaders were mean-spirited old men who would do anything to achieve some political victory. Since then, I couldn't put anything past Republicans, and I have been proved right many times.

Recount! Recount!!

I was in America during the Recount debacle following the year 2000 elections. Those who predicted that the advent of the millennium would bring in chaos would have been right on the money had they picked November as the start of the forecasted problem rather than January 1, 2000. It was sheer chaos.

Then incumbent Vice-President Al Gore was winning the national popular vote, that is, he had the simple majority of American voters voting for him. But the American election system uses what they call the Electoral College to elect the President. Each state had a number of Electoral College votes allotted to it. Except for two states which use a system based on the number of districts won, it is winner-takes-all, that is, if a candidate won the most votes in a state, all the Electoral College votes of that state went to that candidate. When all electoral votes are tallied, whichever candidate had the most Electoral College votes (currently at least 270) would be the new President. As election results started streaming in, it soon became clear that whoever won the 25 electoral votes of the state of Florida would win the US Presidency. At the end of the day, George W. Bush was declared winner, but only by whiskers!

Can you imagine a national election being determined by 537 votes in the most critical state, Florida, in a country of over 300 million people, with thousands of votes discarded, votes that were mainly in the districts that normally voted for the 'losing' side? Many Democrats believe, to this day, that the winner should have been Al Gore and not George W. Bush.

But thank God for the resilience of American institutions, the belief of the general populace in the rule of law, as well as their belief in the fairness and truthfulness of those institutions. What happened in the United States during the 2000 elections would normally lead to serious violence and possibly civil war in many other countries, especially if the contestants were from different ethnic or tribal regions of the country. Well, despite the fact that most Americans are settlers, or descendants of settlers from many lands, once they become Americans, most people see America as their country, relegating, or even cutting off primordial loyalties to their ethnic roots or their land of origin.

What would it have been like if Al Gore was from Ireland and George Bush was from England, and the entire population divided along those lines? What would have happened if you said that Bush won by 537 votes in the most critical state, while at the same time disqualifying thousands of other votes that could have gone to Gore? Or let's say that both were Muslims and Al Gore was Shiite and George Bush was Sunni (come to think of it, a Sunni George Bush does not look too far-fetched – what of all those close ties his family is said to have with the oil Sheiks and the Kingdom of Saudi Arabia). With George Bush declared winner under those circumstances and the populace split up along the Sunni-Shiite divide, it would have been CHAOS. You would still be picking up bomb shrapnel on American streets today.

Remember that in all this, Bill Clinton of the Democratic Party was incumbent President (albeit weakened by the Monica Lewinsky scandal), and the same Al Gore was his Vice-President. Remember that Al Gore was actually Al Gore, Jr. His father, just like George Bush's, was a well-known politician – so he did not come into the contest without strong antecedents. He was the incumbent Vice-President! He and Bill Clinton had had a successful 8-year run at the helm of the Executive branch of the US government, and in his own case, there was no allegation of an involvement with a twenty-something-year-old girl – at least to the best of our knowledge!

You tell me, in which country of the world you would have the incumbent Vice-President lose an election to succeed his boss of 8 years, the President, with 537 vote difference in a country of over 300 million, against someone who had never been in Federal Government! Although George Bush also came into the contest with powerful antecedents (he was a two-time Governor of Texas and had actually lived in the White House while his Father, George H.W. Bush was US President), but these were not considered strong enough to truncate the successful Clinton-Gore Democratic line.

Al Gore could be renamed "The Man Who Was Never To Be President." Things just did not work in his favor. Even when the Supreme Court ruled against him, they said that that ruling must not be referenced in any future court case, ever! Rumor had it that he did not want the then-still-popular Bill Clinton to campaign for him because of the Lewinsky scandal. Well, I wish he had had a chance to see into the future, I wish he had the opportunity to see into 2008 and 2012 and the same Clinton endorsing Barack Obama. Bill Clinton is getting more and more popular with each passing day. And Al Gore? Al Gore becomes Al Gore more and more with each passing day.

The Iraq War – War by All Means

The decision by the Bush Administration to lead America into the Iraq war was like those often taken by the then military Heads of State who ruled Nigeria as I was growing up. When they came out to say that their unelected Supreme Military Council had decided something, they would just issue a decree to make it law.

In a similar way, the decision to go to war against Iraq and overthrow Saddam Hussein had been taken by the "Supreme Presidential Council" of President Bush, Vice-President Dick Cheney, and their inner circle well before it happened. All that was required was to find a good reason for the war and cover it all under a cloak of democracy.

In order to make it legitimate, they had to bring in the United Nations claiming that Iraq possessed weapons of mass destruction (WMDs). In a presentation fronted by General Colin Powell, a man who had had a sterling career and had held his head high up to that point, bogus claims were made by America to justify the war.

Looking back now, you can see how much damage a phony war has done to people everywhere. I felt serious pain each time the deaths of young US servicemen who were just about the age of my son were being reported on TV - especially after it became clear that Iraq had no WMDs. It was really sad that a war that should never have been fought had deprived many families of their children. There are many wounded warriors today from that war, and many people who have been scarred for life. And this is not to talk of the economic disaster the war brought on America.

Even in a democratic setting, leaders can lead the entire nation on the wrong path. The aftermath of the Iraq war has not cleared till this day. Today President George W. Bush is living comfortably and receiving his grandchildren, while the means for many families to have grandchildren has been destroyed forever – just because someone wanted to avenge a dictator's attack against his dad.

Chapter 3

Immigration & Cultural Affinity in America

I realize that every legal immigrant of today was just one step away from becoming an undocumented immigrant, sometime in the past. You only needed to have missed a date by which you should have done something or filed something, and then the whole future comes crashing down for you.

3
Immigration and Cultural Affinity in America

W hen people come to visit from Africa and want to extend their stay beyond the date stamped in their passport, we advise them to write a letter to US Citizenship and Immigration Services (USCIS) requesting an extension and stating why they want their stay extended. Our people become apprehensive, and start to fear that this would give Immigration information about them - where they were staying, when they entered, when they now plan to leave - information they believe would lead the authorities directly to them.

We allay their fears by saying something like: "You came in with a valid visa, you declared where you will be staying to Immigration upon entry, and all you are asking for is a 3-month extension. If Immigration should deny you, what do they want to do about the hundreds of people who just stroll across the US-Mexico border and disappear into thin air daily, with no forwarding addresses? Why would US Immigration refuse your solitary application, in which you are voluntarily declaring your location, purpose of your visit, reason for asking for extension, etc, when many others never had the courtesy of doing that?" Most of such applications are routinely approved by the immigration authorities. In fact, if the extension is given and they still need to stay a little more, we still encourage them to apply for an extended extension.

Immigration has become a major political issue in America. At the last count, there was said to be over 11 million undocumented immigrants living in and breathing the air of various American cities and suburbs. Republican politicians at the national level, especially those from the border states (where the undocumented immigrant populations are huge), always want to talk tough on illegal immigration, even if what they are saying is impracticable or doesn't make sense.

You will notice that I called the immigrants we are talking about "undocumented," and their style of immigration "illegal," because that is what it is. Labels have also become important in discussing these issues. Some politicians call the undocumented "illegal immigrants" or simply "illegals." I refrain from using those labels because, as an immigrant myself, I realize that every legal immigrant of today was just one step away from becoming an undocumented immigrant, sometime in the past. You only needed to have missed a date by which you should have done something or filed something, and then the whole future comes crashing down for you. And that's if you were legal at the beginning.

You see, except for Native American tribes, all Americans are immigrants or descendants of immigrants. In fact, those making laws for the nation on Capitol Hill should check what their forefathers did to achieve "legal immigrant" status. Some might have bribed, some might have forged documents, and some might have been forced to "contract" marriage with US citizens, only God knows. It would be interesting to understand how the parents, grandparents or great-grandparents of today's lawmakers got in here and became "legal." I want to believe that not all of them were squeaky clean, even if the record books haven't captured the unclean parts of their history. There is a proverb that says people living in glass houses should not throw stones. While they make the laws today, they should know that a generation or two ago, they were probably undocumented themselves. Thank God things have changed for them. The actions of some of our lawmakers in Congress today are like the actions of someone who uses a ladder to climb to the top, and then pulls that ladder up so those coming along behind will have no ladder to climb with.

Apart from Native American tribes, the only other people excluded from the immigration debate are the descendants of slaves brought to America against their will and forced to work without compensation. Their forefathers paid too high a price for an immigration they did not seek or want.

In 1994, the US State Department initiated a Diversity Visa (DV) Lottery to "balance" the US population by granting, through a lottery, 54,000 visas yearly to countries under-represented in the American society. It's as if America is a world parliament to which every country should send representatives. This program has worked well, and people who could never have dreamed of coming to live in America are now immigrants. Many of them have now become US citizens.

The USCIS has programs through which an undocumented immigrant who enrolls for US military service can become a US citizen after a couple of years. There are also paths for scientists, artists, athletes and others needed by American society to come in legally and work and live in America. Other people who are legal immigrants today include those who legally obtained work visas before coming here and followed the process to obtain legal immigrant visas.

Bottom line, this is an immigrant society, and there are many proofs to confirm this. Names for example, show where the forefathers may have come from. American names are almost as diverse as the number of countries in the world. You have O'Malley and O'Brien from Ireland, you have Chu, Chen, and Wang from China, you also have Adebayo and Okeke from Nigeria, etc. What we can't glean from these names is what their original bearers (or ancestors) did to become legitimate citizens of the land.

I have also found that America, being a nation of immigrants, is also a nation of multiple accents. Apart from the various accents of immigrants, we find that there is a difference between how someone who grew up in one of the southern states of America speaks compared to someone who grew up in the north. I have also heard that there is a New Jersey accent, a California accent, a Long Island accent, and a Texas accent. I still cannot differentiate them,

Immigrants like me have added to the multiplicity of accents, that the whole country has become a "Babel" of accents. But the good thing is that people speak with their accents without feeling embarrassed. So when someone says to me "I love your accent" I say right back "I love yours too." And when they say "your accent sounds nice, where is it from" I reply "Nigeria, how about yours?"

The poor, the weak and the oppressed

People from different parts of the world tend to concentrate in specific parts of America as they settle down. This happens naturally, as new immigrants need the support of kith and kin already settled in America when they arrive. So when the new immigrants settle, they generally settle in areas where the older immigrants have settled or started businesses.

This is what gave rise to Chinatowns, Little Italy, and similar concentrations of nationalities. People of Irish descent settled in Boston and Brooklyn, while it is common belief that Jewish people own substantial swaths of New York City.

Apart from some Eastern African communities in Minnesota, Africans don't seem to have formed the bond that could make them come together and settle in one place. They are scattered all over the country, as the people of the biblical Babel. You see, even back in Africa, there is little bonding between tribes within and outside national boundaries. Differences in languages and culture make them as non-cohesive with each other as with people of Caucasian roots. The only difference is that all black people bond together when there is racial injustice meted out to one of them or when there is hope for one of them to rise above the rest to exalted heights – just to prove the black race too is not always meant for the basement. This was clearly demonstrated in the election of Barack Obama as US president in 2008. Black people who never cared about voting actually came out to vote – regardless of the politics of Barack Obama or that of the Democratic Party. African-American churches bussed people to voting centers, despite the fact that the Democratic Party which Obama represented was pro-abortion, while churches are largely anti-abortion. I do not have the statistics, but if you check, you would find that many black Republicans (of whatever number of them that exist) would have voted for Barack Obama.

It is a natural instinct, which has been there from the beginning of time. Despite their differences, the poor band together when it comes to the matters of the rich, and the weak band together when it comes to the matters of the strong. This has been borne out by history and has been the theme of many movies and literary works. Regardless of the political posturing and political correctness of the day, the truth of history is that the black man in America has been poor, weak and has suffered oppression, and, more importantly, sees himself in those lights. Even those who have made it among them are not blind to this historical reality.

How do you want your steak?

As people are diverse in America, so is the food. Thanks to America, I've eaten in Indian restaurants without going to India and I've eaten in Thai restaurants without going to Thailand. Chinese restaurants are all over the place, and Italian food is in most restaurants. There are several Mexican restaurants, Vietnamese restaurants, Greek restaurants, Moroccan restaurants, etc. And of course, there are a few African (i.e. black African) restaurants where you can eat foofoo, and, if you like, eat with your fingers instead of a fork and knife without anyone staring at you. So while still in America, you may very well travel the world by the way of food!

African food and the way it is prepared is as diverse as the tribes and language groups of Africa are diverse. We had a number of Kenyans in our Church some years ago. During a Church picnic, some Nigerian members brought cooked beef.

In Nigeria and along the West African coast, beef is cut into pieces, sometimes as big as a man's fist. Then, it is boiled until it is very well-cooked and eatable. After this, it is grilled, fried, or cooked in a pot of stew, so by the time you eat it, you are eating well-cooked meat.

The Kenyan brothers later told me they were initially very skeptical of eating the Nigerian-prepared meat. Why? They informed me that in Kenya, beef is cut up into tiny pieces, of about the size of game dice, then boiled and cooked. Looking at the fist-sized Nigerian-prepared meat, they believed there was no way it could be cooked well enough inside. It took a lot of courage for them to try it, nibbling from the edges, but to their surprise, the fist-sized pieces were very well-cooked.

Then there is the issue of steak served in restaurants. This is served as well-done, medium, or rare. When steak is sliced for you at an office party or restaurant, you see bloody fluid streaming from the steak. This horrifies Africans, because they believe the meat was not well-cooked. So look out at those company parties, Africans there are not likely to partake of the steak if it is not well cooked or is oozing traces of blood. When an African orders steak in a restaurant and the waiter asks: "how do you want it: medium, rare or well-done?" You are most likely to hear the African say "well-done" in response. Medium or rare just doesn't cut it, pardon the pun.

The question still remains: when people in "civilized" nations are able to eat "rare" or "medium"-cooked steak which oozes bloody fluid on the plate, who then is the savage?

The Forerunners

Africans have only in the last few decades started making the US their immigration destination. Being a former British colony, Nigerians used to flood into Britain to settle more than they came to the US. On the other hand, people from other countries had been immigrating to America for several generations. We see a lot of Americans today who are of Indian and Chinese descent, some in the second, third, or fourth generations.

During the technology boom of the 1990s, many people of Indian origin immigrated to the US to work in the area of computer technology. They got jobs here on the basis of their skills and experience. I think that one of the things that made it easier for them was that there is a large pool of technically skilled people back in India, and also that, like Nigeria, India was a former British colony, and English is an official language. So communication is not a serious obstacle, and transition of their skills into America was smooth. The result is that most of the non-immigrant work visas issued yearly are snapped up by people coming from Asia.

In today's world, where national boundaries have shrunk and the world is now a global village, it is really a good thing for young people to learn disciplines and obtain qualifications that can be easily migrated across borders – a Skills-Without-Borders kind of thing.

Somehow, people from India and China who have been living in the US for a long time have established firm roots in America. Many are in information technology, medicine, banking, and mass media, and we hear of quite a number who have been very successful as politicians. For example, Governor Nikki Haley, an Indian-American, is the first woman to serve as Governor of South Carolina. In Louisiana, Bobby Jindal, another Indian-American is Governor and is constantly rumored to be a possible candidate for US President.

We also find that many of the Dunkin Donut shops are owned and manned by people from India, who are also believed to own many 7-Eleven stores as well as many Sunoco and Exxon gas stations.

The way I see it as an immigrant is that these are people who have dreamed the American Dream and have done something about it. They overcame obstacles and are now part of the American story. They became successful not because anyone handed them favors, and not because people had pity on them.

This must be the goal and focus of every immigrant - to work hard, aim for success, avoid distractions, hold tenaciously to their vision, and in the end achieve the American Dream.

Chapter 4

Politics in America

Many immigrants believe that the main thing the Tea Party rose up to fight was the very idea that a minority had the temerity to occupy the White House, as if all he did was rent the place through a realtor.

4
Politics in America

Republicans versus Democrats

Politics in America are quite interesting. The battle is constantly drawn between the Republican Party (or GOP) and the Democratic Party. Since I arrived in America, I have observed closely the practice of US politics, and I have followed closely the actions of the political institutions and politicians. On every election night, I have stayed up to the wee hours of the next morning, following the reporting and returns of election results until the balance of power in Congress is determined, both during the midterm and general elections.

I am not a member of the Republican Party or the Democratic Party. I have, in the past, voted for Republican candidates and Democrat candidates, based on issues and personalities of the candidates.

In my opinion, stemming from the values settling African immigrants came into America with, many might not be flooding into the US Republican Party and I will tell you why.

You see, from what we could glean from news reports and the pronouncements of their leaders, the Republican Party agenda seems to be only about themselves. The Republican attitude is like this:

"This is our pie. Our fore-fathers baked it and left it for us. We will eat it to our satisfaction and will not share it with anyone."

Or

"This is my pie. I have worked hard for it. Only me, my wife and my children can taste of it. Whatever remains after we are full we will donate to the Museum of the Dead so that no living person will eat from it. Let everyone who wants to eat pie bake their own pie."

From what I have seen, taking care of the less privileged in society is anathema to the Republican Party. They want to do away with welfare programs for the poor, they want to eliminate or cut down spending on Medicare and Medicaid, food stamps, social security, unemployment benefits, etc. They variously describe these benefits as "socialism," "communism," and "entitlement," and every Republican candidate for office campaigns on cancelling every public assistance funding, some of them describing the recipients of such welfare packages as "lazy."

You see, in the African society where I grew up, when you are successful, you and the rest of the society believe that your success is a blessing from God - that it is not the amount of work that one does that makes one rich, and we have many idioms and proverbs that support this. Make no mistake, laziness and stealing have no place and are roundly condemned in the African community where I grew up. People don't pity the lazy or the thief. But not being successful after doing the right things does not send you to the dog house in Africa!

There is a saying: One rich person and six destitute people in a family still make that family a poor family. The moral is that a rich man has not attained real riches until he helps lift the fortunes of some other members of the family. It is only when this happens that the family is considered rich. Helping the poor and the less privileged is woven into the fabric of the communal African society in which I grew up. This is what US Republicans hate.

In addition, you don't find many African-Americans in leadership in the Republican Party. The Republican Party seems to be more of a WHITE party than the Democratic Party. It is among them that you will find the fringe elements of the land: the staunch, die-hard, white supremacists, and the white-only elements of the American society: the Aryan groups, the neo-Nazis, and the so-called "rednecks." As far as these fringe groups are concerned, all the minority races of America come from some sub-species of the human race.

But Republican politicians, in my view, are smarter and better at political maneuverings than Democrats. You only need to watch the HBO movie RECOUNT (based on the 2000 US elections) to understand the political astuteness of the Republicans. They manipulated the officials that could be manipulated, bought those who could be bought, bulldozed their way around, made all the right noises, cried out in agony even when they were wrong, and they got 8 years of George W. Bush's presidency to show for it!

At the time Republicans were doing all this, Democrats, led by their Presidential candidate Al Gore and their party officials, were playing the nice guys around the country, acting like they were only in Florida for the Fair Play Trophy, waiting for an umpire to magically appear and hand them the medal for the "best behaved team," and not caring that the opposing team was walking away with the trophy and gold medal. In that contest, Republicans showed Democrats that nice guys in politics usually don't get on the winner's podium, and that only those who win the war live to write the history.

In my own view, Democratic Party strategists look like cub scouts beside Republican Party strategists.

The Evangelicals

There is this group of Republican Evangelicals who speak for all US Evangelicals, and the Republican Party embraces them as another column of the party. Many Africans settling in the US are Christians, and many of them are truly born-again evangelical Christians. Many African church groups have also established strong, virile, evangelical church-es in the United States, and many have large congregations. The Republican Evangelicals hold many Bible-backed posi-tions, like being anti-abortion and not supporting gay mar-riage. Immigrant Evangelicals settling in America hold these same positions too.

However, there are many African people, many of them Evangelicals, who may not join the Republican Party, because some of the Republican values affect, not just the evangelical viewpoints, but also the economic and social relationship of the people. The foundational principle of the Republican Party, which seems to be "everyone for himself," is completely opposite to the African communal spirit, where everyone is concerned about the well-being of every other person in the community. Everyone who does honest work but may still be unfortunate in the results is not considered lazy and indo-lent by the rest of the community. You help them when they are out of work, without thinking of them as leeches. This is why homelessness as we know it in the USA does not exist in many African societies.

The basic mindset of the average person who grew up in that traditional environment is to take care of their kin and the less-privileged in the society. These were the very princi-ples that Jesus taught:

Then the King will say to those on His right hand,

"Come, you blessed of my Father, inherit the kingdom prepared for you from the foundation of the world: for I was hungry and you gave me food; I was thirsty and you gave me drink; I was a stranger and you took me in; I was naked and you clothed me; I was sick and you visited me; I was in prison and you came to me."

Then the righteous will answer Him, saying, "Lord, when did we see you hungry and feed you, or thirsty and give you drink? When did we see you a stranger and take you in, or naked and clothe you? Or when did we see you sick, or in prison, and come to you?"

And the King will answer and say to them, "Assuredly, I say to you, inasmuch as you did it to one of the least of these my brethren, you did it to me." (Matthew 25:34-40 NKJV).

Africans had been practicing these principles long before Europeans brought Christianity to Africa, and before the first copy of the Bible entered the continent. I believe that the leadership of US evangelical churches stand for these principles as much as the immigrant Evangelicals are standing for them. Not so much so among Republicans.

What you see in America today is a section of the entire evangelical spectrum, mainly immigrants, who are opposed to gay marriage and abortion, but who are forced to stand with the Democratic Party because of their ideas of helping people with low incomes, supporting welfare spending, and low income housing. They do so because, in these areas, the Republican ideas are rather unwelcoming and contradict some of the beliefs of these Evangelicals. More importantly, some of these immigrant Evangelicals, or their friends, or members of their extended family are recipients of these benefits. They therefore cannot relate to the Republican Party positions in these areas.

The best solution would probably be a third political party emerging in the future that holds the best of both worlds: not embracing abortion or gay marriage, but supporting welfare spending and other social programs. You would see the ranks of Republican Evangelicals diminishing as people would swarm to the new party.

It should be noted therefore that the known Evangelicals in the US who speak for the Republican Party might not be speaking for all American Evangelicals. The immigrant Evangelicals have their own voices, and may be speaking a different tune loudly at the ballot boxes.

Remember we said that the African ideal is taking care of your brother, and the less-privileged in the family, and, by extension, society? As we have seen, this is more of a Democratic Party idea than a Republican Party one. So each year, thousands of Africans are settling in the US along with their children - both those brought here, and those born here. These children are becoming doctors, engineers, lawyers, scientists and educators in American society, and are growing up with the same ideas as their parents. These children and their parents will no doubt participate in shaping the future of American society.

Also, as I have witnessed in my lifetime, historically, US Presidents from the Democratic Party stand up for the developing world more than Republican Presidents. We knew more of President Carter (and his Secretary of State Andrew Young), and later President Bill Clinton in Nigeria than we did of Presidents Nixon, Ford, and George H. W. Bush combined. Democratic leaders have also supported the civil rights agenda more than Republicans. History cannot forget the position of the United States under Republican President Reagan on apartheid in South Africa, a position that remained until very late in the day.

For these and many other reasons, the Democratic Party seems to be more of a natural path for settling Africans. If this pattern holds, just look down the road at the next ten years, and see what the compositions of the parties will be.

With all these said, what makes the future even more frightening for the Republican Party is that there is a huge population of undocumented, mostly Hispanic immigrants living in America today. Sooner or later, this chunk of society will be formally absorbed into America under one legislative framework or another. They will change the face of America, and Spanish will become the second language of commerce.

This is already the case in some states and it is appearing in other states.

In the Hispanic family system, they look out for each other and support each other, as Africans do. You may ask yourself, how did 11 million people keep on finding homes in America over the years without needing to sleep under bridges? It was because those already here took them in and helped them settle. They did not see them as leeches, but as people they had a responsibility to help.

Politics is a game of numbers. In the 2012 elections, the Hispanic population mostly sided with Democrats. When you add the immigrant African populations and their offspring, and tack on the soon-to-be-documented Hispanic population (or their children), the Republican Party might find themselves struggling where they shouldn't. If steps are not taken, it will just be a matter of time.

How Republicans Can Court Immigrants

In my own opinion, the Republican Party has many good things going for it. For example, it is among Republicans that you find people who still believe in God in America. The people who believe in Creation are in the Republican Party although they are constantly derided by evolutionists. You see, Africans have the idea of, and belief in the Creator and in God (or gods) "woven into their DNA", so to say, from birth. This is a good starting point for the Republican Party.

However, the current Republican positions on welfare programs for the poor, on Medicare and Medicaid, food stamps, and other public assistance spending will always be an obstacle to African immigrants joining the Party. Their proportions in the populace may be different, but there are poor people of all races in America. Republicans need to stand up for the poor of America and make the necessary laws and provide funding for their welfare.

We have said that Bible-believing Americans are in the Republican Party. The Bible actually says:

"For the poor will never cease from the land; therefore I command you, saying, 'You shall open your hand wide to your brother, to your poor and your needy, in your land.'" (Deuteronomy 15:11, NKJV)

Also, when there is senseless killing of African-Americans especially in the hands of the police – which happens often - you hardly hear the voices of the Republican Party leadership, you only hear Democrats. Yet I am sure that Republican leaders don't support extra-judicial killings. It will be good if Republican leaders join their voices to the calls for justice for the victims.

It will also be helpful if the Party leadership at all levels distance themselves from the fringe elements of the Party, and not make them seem to be speaking for the entire Republican Party, as it often appears to be. Prominent fringe elements say that African-Americans should go back to Africa, among many other racial insults. Really? In 2014? The Republican leadership must stand up and state the Party position against such expressions of racial bias.

The Tea Party and Other Partisans

When the first African-American President was elected in 2008, Fox News led the opposition against Barack Obama. Some people, unable to tolerate the idea of a black man in the White House, started querying the legitimacy of Barack Obama as President, contending that he was not born in the USA. That controversy has not subsided to this day. It became a movement of its own, and people with this idea have become known as "birthers" or "truthers" - making the rest of us "liars" in the spirit of those words. One of the qualifications to be President in the USA is to be a native-born American, so those of us who naturalized are automatically ruled out of ruling from the White House.

Fox News anchors and journalists gave the "birthers" and their agenda the visibility and the reach they needed. The chorus of the "birthers" was joined by the Libertarian groups, of which the Tea Party Movement became the most prominent. The Libertarians tout the Constitution as the most authentic document to govern American lives and they throw this in your face, as if every other American is anti-Constitution, and as if, while they believe in the Constitution as the basis for governance, the rest of us believe in some other document delivered from Mars or Jupiter.

It is pathetic that the Tea Party takes only what is useful to them from the US Constitution, and jettison the rest for a day that should never come. Remember that the rise of the "birthers" and the rise of the Tea party happened around the same time. The Tea Party platform helped some people vent their discomfort with the idea of a black President. While it would be seen as insensitive to openly support the "birthers," some elected Republicans openly supported the Tea Party. At their rallies, they portrayed Barack Obama variously as an African witch doctor, or as a monkey, among several demeaning and insulting posters. The message was clear: having a black man as President in the White House was too insulting to their egos.

As Democratic strategist Paul Begala said on CNN recently, "the Tea Party folks hate Barack Obama as the devil hates holy water." Many immigrants believe that the main thing the Tea Party rose up to fight was the very idea that a minority had the temerity to occupy the White House, as if all he did was rent the place through a realtor. They forget that he received his mandate for the keys of the White House through popular vote in an open election and with the assent of the majority of American voters.

Yet it is the same Constitution they tout that guaranteed Barack Obama could be President of the United States of

America. If they believed the Constitution, they should have seen him as just another American whose time had come. All that was needed was proof he was born in the United States. The State of Hawaii confirmed that Barack Obama was born there and even went as far as releasing his birth certificate. The argument should have ended there. But no, a million birth certificates would not satisfy them. What they probably needed was a chemical reaction to change the skin color of this new White House occupant. It is so shameful that some well-known, but small-minded people like Donald Trump joined the "birthers," and even some members of Congress overtly supported them.

I have heard fellow immigrants say that only a bastard African-American would ever join the "birthers" or the Tea Party, because their agenda was clear. I actually thought of it and concluded, based on what we knew of the Tea Party and the "birthers," that they would be unable to get African-Americans join their ranks. Lo and behold, a few days later, I saw on TV a couple of African-Americans at a Tea Party rally and I could not help but shake my head and mutter just one word to myself over and over again........

After Obama became President, I am sure some "birthers" and Tea Party members would have rushed back into the history books and other documents to review the Hawaii Admission Act of 1959 and to see if it could be faulted in any way. They would have scrutinized in 2008 the 1959 statehood of Hawaii to see if it could be invalidated If they had found a way to invalidate it, that would have meant that Hawaii was not a legitimate state of the USA, and that would have made Obama not to have been born in the United States, making his presidency illegal, and the "birthers," the Tea Party and the Republicans would have held unending celebrations.

I say to them: don't tell me about the Constitution if you only pick and choose what is convenient for you!

And while all this was going on, Republican leaders remained silent, fuelling the Tea Party beneath the surface, and hoping that one day, a national movement would succeed in unseating Obama. But the majority of America backed "the skinny kid with the funny name," and even re-elected him for a second term in 2012.

Chapter 5

Race in America

Anytime a policeman goes beyond subduing an unarmed person and takes a life, the policeman has made himself the accuser, the prosecutor, the jury, and the judge, and that is too much power for anyone in America!

5
Race in America

R ace will always be an issue in America - there isn't
anything anyone can do to stop racial biases.

In the course of my career in the United States,
I have worked with many hard-working and brilliant white
colleagues who were recognized and promoted for their skills
and accomplishments. I have also worked with a number of
lazy and inept white colleagues who believed that they should
be recognized and rewarded over every black employee (including yours truly), just because they were white, without
regard to our different abilities, responsibilities, and results. In
all my years working in America, I have received promotions
and recognitions under many race-neutral bosses, and had
the misfortune of one boss that was race-partial.

I found it easy to relate to my colleagues because I did
not relate to them based on skin color. I did not see them as
white or black. As I did not see anyone in the light of their
skin color, I was not intimidated by anyone, nor did I hold
anyone in awe. I believed that corporate America would
not employ someone for the fun of it, and certainly not for

charity at the level at which I was working. I saw each of my colleagues as people bringing something valuable to the table. My view, however, was not universal.

There were a few people who believed that your ideas had to be wrong just because it was your idea, would not evaluate the merit of it, and looked down on you because you were not white. The good thing was if you had a result or solution-minded boss, they would most likely go with the best idea on the table, no matter whose idea it was. They would not play games with business solutions on the basis of race. This kind of boss got results and motivated employees. Fortunately, most bosses I worked with fell into this category, and this is the general trend in corporate America.

I personally believe that the majority of white Americans are not racists, and everywhere you go, you meet people who treat you as an equal. But there are also people who will always treat you different. They don't hurt you, but they don't accept you either. Then there is a minority who feel that because you are black, you cannot, and should not, attempt to respond or speak to an issue, just because of your skin color. They display an air of superiority and believe they are better than you, just because they are white. Such people always look stupid and childish to me. If they keep this belief to themselves, it might be pardonable, but they flaunt it and want you to believe it too. If you probe further, they are usually just noise.

Some people believe that when a black person excels, it is a stroke of luck that could not be repeated, just like lightning is said not to strike in the same place twice. My attitude has always been to work hard and make sure that the lightning strikes more than 20 times at the same place! My goal is to prove to them this inalienable truth - all men are created equal.

The Police May NOT Be Your Friend

While I find the police and other law enforcement responsible for the safety of life and property in America, the average white policeman is more likely to be racially-biased against black people. White policemen always present a definite dislike for the average black man. They act so unfriendly that I wonder who coined the phrase: "the police is your friend." Most policemen I've spoken with talked to me roughly, even when there was no need for it. There was a time I was involved in a minor fender bender and the policeman who was there taking statements was barking orders at me very harshly for no reason, and afterwards went to speak to the other party – a white man and his wife, in a normal, civil tone.

I worked for 7 years in New Jersey, and of all the states I have passed through, New Jersey police are probably the most racist policemen in America, followed closely by those in Texas. They look out for you, and the moment they notice a black driver, they become energized. You see the way they engage their patrol cars - it's like when a lion or leopard makes the move to jump on its prey.

There was a time I was coming down Delaware Memorial Bridge into New Jersey. The officer in the wide median divide at the bottom of the bridge was not making a move to pursue anyone until I passed him. If it was for speed, which he claimed it was, his radar would have picked me up well before I came alongside his patrol car, and he would have been making the motions to come after me. It was when I looked across, and our eyes met that he decided to come after me. There was another time that I was stopped by police for driving 30 mph in a 45 mph zone in New Jersey! The officer said I was driving too slowly – on a rural road!

In Texas, I had similar experiences as in New Jersey. The additional problem I saw in Texas was that, seeing your license is from another state, they would give you a hefty ticket fine, knowing you would not be able to come to court to contest it.

These experiences were not unique to me as friends and colleagues who reside in Texas, Delaware, New Jersey and Pennsylvania and have fallen prey to them have shared similar stories. For full disclosure, all these corroborators are black.

It is a fact that a disproportionate majority of arrested criminals are black. Perhaps this is the reason policemen put a blanket label of "criminal" on every black person. You see, according to the Bureau of Justice Statistics published by the US Department of Justice, as of December 31, 2010 there were:

- 3,074 Black male prisoners per 100,000 Black male US residents.

- 1,258 Hispanic male prisoners per 100,000 Hispanic male US residents.

- 459 White male prisoners per 100,000 White male US residents.

This means that there were 3 black men in prison for every 100 black men in America!

So out of 100 black families, these were three families where the father was not there to support the mother, the son had no father-figure, and the daughter had no one in her life to keep predators at bay and guide her to success. With the father being in jail and the mother struggling to put food on the table, children are exposed to all sorts of negative pressures and distractions. This is the problem of single parenthood and it is the root of teenage pregnancy. This is also the root of drugs and violence, leading the next generation straight into prison.

However, as grim as these statistics are, they should not justify the hostility and the extra-judicial killings that police in different parts of America perpetrate against black people and other minorities on a regular basis. These are just too prevalent. There is a black man or the other being killed by the use of excessive force almost every day. Unless they really aim to take a man's life, a trained policeman should not need to pump 10 bullets into a person to subdue him, even if they saw him with a weapon. What do they teach them in the police academy anyway?

And then you have the case of four policemen shooting down a defenseless young black man who had no weapon, each pumping 8 or 10 bullets into this person, as if their guns were on auto-fire. Anytime this happens, it should be classified as murder. One person firing his gun is more than enough, and he does not need to fire 10 shots to subdue someone. Unless the black person is being used for target practice, two or three or four policemen firing multiple shots at one person is murder and they should be prosecuted. I think that their goal is to make sure the victim does not live to tell his side of the story, so they fire excessive shots to permanently silence him.

And in every one of these cases, the police department comes out to defend the injustice. No policeman is handcuffed and put behind bars pending investigation. Every trigger-happy policeman therefore receives some "immunity" immediately after murdering a defenseless young black man, unless the case is pursued and an indictment is brought up. There is no deterrence, no caution, and the next policeman is just waiting to summarily execute the next black man.

Two examples come to mind. In February 1999, an unarmed, 23-year-old immigrant from Guinea, Amadou Diallo, was shot and killed by four New York City Police officers outside his apartment in the Bronx, New York. They fired a combined total of 41 shots at Diallo, 19 of which struck him. FORTY-ONE shots. At the end of the trial all four were acquitted. In November, 2006, three unarmed black men were shot at a total of fifty times (yes FIFTY) by a team of NYPD officers, killing one of them, Sean Bell, on the morning before his wedding, and severely wounding the other two. At the end of the day, the 3 officers that were tried (on charges ranging from manslaughter to reckless endangerment) were found not guilty. In case after case, it is being established that the lives of young black men are cheap in America.

It becomes increasingly difficult to exonerate the judiciary from complicity when you look at these cases. I don't have the statistics, but I read somewhere that the punishment for possessing cocaine (which poor black people cannot afford) is much lighter than the punishment for crack (a drug cheap enough for poor black folks to get). Who made these laws?

And speaking of the judiciary, the issue of probation sentences given by judges needs to be looked into, especially for young black men. How do you give an 18-year old person a 5-year probation sentence? At 18 years, you are at the peak of making the most mistakes you will make in life. With probation hanging in the air, any mistake will definitely send them to jail for a long time. If a young man is given this kind of probation, it should be accompanied by mandatory classes and continuous counseling. Leaving them to themselves is like setting a time bomb, and pronto, the young man adds to the prison population.

If a black man shoots a white man in cold blood, he is definitely bound for the gallows, definitely bound for prison, and probably to a life in prison. If, on the other hand, a white man shoots a black man in cold blood, nothing is definite. It depends on the police. It depends on the prosecutor. It depends on the judge. It depends on the jury. It depends on the witnesses. It depends on the county. It depends on the state. It depends on the victim's criminal history. It depends on so many things that you wonder if it is the same system of justice that we're talking about.

After the Diallo killing in 1999, I called my son and told him that whenever any policeman accosts him, he should always raise his hands and never argue, even if the policeman is unreasonable or hostile. I taught him that America has placed little value on the lives of young black men. I taught him what I learned from a Bob Marley song in my college days in Nigeria: he who fights and runs away, lives to RUN another day (Bob Marley said FIGHT, I say RUN). You see, in order to amount to anything in America, you have to be alive, and it is my desire for each of my children to amount to something.

With all these killings, you wonder why the US State Department should have the audacity to protest extra-judicial killings by some tyrant in some backward country of the world, while black American youth are routinely sent to the great beyond by American policemen. This is not to say tyrants and murderers should have free rein. I am against every form of injustice in every part of the world, including inside the USA. I'm just saying - physician, heal thyself!

What's to be done?

While black people have had a rough beginning in America, there needs to be a deliberate way to move black youth into a new era and a new day. Black leaders need to do more than the occasional protest when another black young man is senselessly shot by a white racist, or when trigger-happy policemen pump more bullets into an unarmed black man than is needed to kill a herd of elephants.

Black leaders need to organize and develop programs to help build the self-esteem of black youth, from very early ages. There should be widespread programs that teach black youth responsibility and safe living in society. There should be programs showing young black people what black people have achieved in America and in the world – in education, sciences and the arts, and not just in basketball or rap music. Take them on exchange programs to Africa and let them spend some time among other black children in good schools in safe areas. Let them aspire to be more than they see in rap music videos. If this is done, we would have a generation of motivated black youth who aspire to be more and reach for the stars.

The cycle of poverty, drugs, single parenthood, teenage motherhood and violence (whether black-on-black or any other type) to which black youth are constantly exposed disorients them and prevents them from reaching the same kind of potential their white classmates are able to reach. What happens in black communities in America today is a cycle that had been repeating itself over and over again since the black man was emancipated and received voting rights – and it has to stop. If the government uses part of its welfare expenditure to fund motivational programs transparently organized by black leaders, educators, activists and intellectuals, the black youth becoming adults in the next 5 to 10 years would have a different focus and aspiration.

Most important, police organizations all over America need to seriously re-orient their officers to regard the lives of all Americans as precious. The goal of a police officer facing a suspected criminal should be to subdue the suspect and bring him to justice, not to kill him. Only in war is a person's goal to kill, and wars are fought by soldiers and marines, not policemen. Americans are not at war at home, and policemen need to stop looking at young black men as enemies to be killed.

Anytime a policeman goes beyond subduing an unarmed person and takes a life, the policeman has made himself the accuser, the prosecutor, the jury, and the judge, and that is too much power for anyone in America! That policeman should be immediately arrested and prosecuted.

Al-Qaeda wants to kill Americans, ISIS wants to kill Americans, the Taliban wants to kill Americans, why on earth should the police in America want to kill Americans?

One thing I taught my children (and the children of other immigrant African families) is that, as a black person, they have the deck stacked against them.

1. First, they are black. This is a disadvantage when dealing with people who are prejudiced against black people: prejudiced bosses, prejudiced employers, prejudiced policemen, prejudiced judges, and prejudiced educators. These are everywhere and you don't know when you will fall into their hands.

2. Second, they speak (at least initially) with an accent. Immigrant Africans and most African-Americans speak with a different accent than white Americans. So when an African-American calls an establishment, the call recipient immediately has an idea of the race of the caller. The neutrality from that point forward depends solely on the race of the call recipient and his or her disposition to racial prejudice.

3. Third: they are foreigners. Their parents may have a

green card, some other work visa, or no valid visa at all. This makes legal matters much more complicated and life more tenuous.

4. They are regarded as outsiders and have to work their way into society.

The Standing Boxer

There is a story of a Nigerian boxer that I told my children on their arrival in America in 1998. This boxer, Peter Konyegwachie, was doing well and came to compete in the 1984 Los Angeles Olympics. He got to the Olympic finals, facing an American called Meldrick Taylor. For both sides, a lot was at stake. While it was the first attempt by the USA to win a gold medal at that division since 1924, it was Nigeria's first chance to win a gold medal in any division in boxing (or in any Olympics sport for that matter). The fight was close, and as it progressed, the American commentator wondered if that gold medal wasn't going to Nigeria, based on Peter's sterling performance.

At the end of the fight, Peter was jumping up and raised his hands in the ring, believing he had won. As we watched in Nigeria, we too believed that he had won and we were rejoicing already. When the decision was handed down, it was a unanimous 5-0 victory for Meldrick Taylor. We felt cheated. Even the American TV commentator said that he didn't think that the fight was that clear cut.

The Nigerian delegation was said to have protested what they called "obvious robbery," but to no avail. If you had the tape and watch the fight, you might also come to the conclusion that a five-zero verdict was unjustified, and a win for Peter was more probable.

Truly the fight was very close, but because both boxers were standing on their feet at the end, the judges scored the fight as they deemed fit – in favor of the American. Could you imagine if Peter had put in extra effort with each punch, stretched himself a little more with each blow, and just put a little more into the fight than the other guy? If Taylor, at the end of the fight, was lying flat on his back on the canvas, then would the fight have been given to him?

THE LESSON? Fight so hard the other guy is not standing on his feet at the end of the fight. I taught my children they have to struggle more and do more than their American colleagues in order to come out indisputably on top. This means, both in school and at the workplace, they need to put in more effort so their work cannot be disparaged, cannot be discarded, and cannot be maligned. While the example I used was from boxing, it is applicable to every sphere of life.

At work, the closing time was 4 p.m. but the earliest I left on any day was 5 p.m. I have stayed back to work till 8 p.m. when I had more to do. You cannot aim to equal what your American colleague is doing and expect to be ranked higher than him. If you do that, you will never be judged better than him because the contest is not always judged fairly. You must always put in more so you always remain a contender for the top. I taught my children this is the only way they can be sure of winning in the American society.

How may I help you?

It's not funny being black in America. When, as a black man, you enter certain stores, a store attendant walks over to you and says: "can I help you find something?" (TRANSLATION: give me the opportunity to stay close to you all the time you are in our store to ensure you don't shop-lift). If you stay long enough and are watchful, you will see that this offer is only extended to black shoppers! Since I learned that, I made up my mind that I would never accept this demeaning offer, even when I really needed help navigating a store. Even if different store attendants ask me that question five times in a day, I will not accept the offer. I prefer to give them a run for their money as they scramble after me all over the store to "prevent" or "monitor" me from committing a shop-lifting that I knew I would never do.

Sometimes, when you are walking on the road and approaching a car with a white person inside, you see the occupant look at you furtively and lock the door. In that case, I move as if I was coming directly at them, looking straight into their eyes as if I had bad intentions. The question is: why should you assume that I would be a mugger and not someone like yourself – someone afraid of being mugged – by both white men and black men?

Some people just cannot see that, despite the fact that you are black, it is quite possible for you to have a similar outlook on life as they do. They cannot imagine that you have the same fears they have, that you desire to do an honest day's work for an honest day's pay as they do, and you want to have a nice, safe time with your family, just as they do. They believe you would do what they would not do. They think the color of your skin changes your heart, your mentality, or the color of the blood running in your veins. If you push the argument further, it seems to suggest that they consider you less of a human being than they are just because you are black.

I come from a country where everyone is black - the millionaires are black, the bank executives are black, the college professors are black, the journalists are black, the fund managers are black, all the Senators are black, the TV anchors are black, the Supreme Court justices are all black, the prisoners are black and even the President has always been black. I therefore take it as a great insult for anyone to infer in any way that I am a lesser human being just because of the color of my skin.

As I was growing up in Africa, it was natural for me to see all successful people as black people. Before coming to America, all the successful people I knew were black, and being black to me has never represented failure, gang life, prison, or inferiority. For me, there's nothing special about being successful and black, just like there's nothing special about being successful and white. Not all white people are successful, just as not all black people are successful. White does not equal success, and black does not equal failure. Black to me is normal, and white is just another color the great Creator God made humans in. To slap a whole race of people with a label and treat all of them as inferior is an insult to their Creator.

There is a school in West Philadelphia which I entered about 7 years ago. It was a predominantly black school in a predominantly black, and difficult neighborhood. There was a mural painted on the wall, presumably to encourage the students to aspire to become something "great." It was a drawing of a welder, an electrician, an EMT technician, a policeman, etc. but no drawing of a Professor, a doctor, an astronaut, or an engineer. Somehow, someone had placed a limitation on what those children could achieve. Those children would end up aspiring to the same level that did not help their parents. Whoever painted that mural certainly did not expect any of those children to work in senior positions at NASA or teach in colleges.

If the same mural was to be painted in a predominantly white school in a white neighborhood, you wouldn't have a welder, electrician, EMT technician, or policeman painted in it. You would have great professions depicted.

The N-word

While the issues of slavery and the civil rights era are mostly gone, the memories linger. And whether you are an African-American or a settling immigrant, you only need to watch the History Channel in February (during the Black History Month) for it all to come back to you. That is why a white person calling a black person a "nigger" (the N-word) always fans a fresh fire.

I still wonder why some African-Americans, especially musicians, actors, comedians and the like are still able to look each other in the face and say the N-word and laugh about it. That word, from all I have read and know, is not a term for endearment or affection. Every time that word was used, it connoted the dehumanization of black people.

In all my years in America, I have never heard immigrant Africans call each other or any black person the N-word. It is just unnatural and abnormal to so do. Why would you call yourself or your brother a name that people only call you derogatorily, a name that transports you back to the years when a black peson was deemed by society not to be 100% a human being?

As it is not right for whites to say the N-word, it is also not right for blacks to say it. It was some people's sweat, tears, blood, and bruises. It was some people's lives.

The sad thing is that the people who popularize the vulgar use of the N-word, those who feel they must utter the N-word with every breath they take are the ones who have achieved some level of success in the society. The way I see it, it seems that they feel that the success they have achieved confers on them certain rights that others do not have. They seem to feel that they have acquired the right to bastardize their heritage, and they do it with impunity. As they spread the N-word around to sweeten their conversations and performances, they forget that the whole of America is listening. When they now hear of a white American using the N-word, they want to have his head, even if he was quoting them verbatim.

I salute those who have made money in the African-American community who are paying it forward, those who remember where they rose from, and who are doing something so that younger people coming behind will have an easier life and better opportunities.

Success is not only measured by gold teeth and long gold chains. It is not measured by expensive cars and outrageous behaviors. Someone who makes money and does not positively affect the community with their money through concrete projects that outlive them, is not living a worthy life.

Chapter 6

The Fourth Estate
of What?

Fox News, though privately owned and funded, turned out to not be the independent, unbiased press organization I expected. To me, Fox News is the headquarters of the Publicity and Information Dissemination Office of the US Republican Party.

6

The Fourth Estate of What?

The Media and Political Partisanship in America

As a young man in Nigeria, I used to wonder why The Guardian (a mostly independent Nigerian newspaper based in Lagos) would report something one way, while the Nigerian Tribune (based in Ibadan and supporting Western Nigeria politicians) would report it a different way, and the New Nigerian (based in Kaduna but supporting Northern Nigeria politicians) would report it in yet another way.

To me, it was political partisanship, which should not be found in the hallowed portals of the news room. I thought only a stupid press would show bias. After all, the populace would see through their partisanship and consider them unreliable as a source of news, opinions and information.

The press, at least from what I knew in Nigeria, always

prided itself as the fourth pillar on which the nation rests, hence the euphemism "the fourth estate of the realm." Growing up, there was incessant demand for freedom of speech and for freedom of the press, from students and other pressure groups. I always sympathized with those demands as I believed that where the press was not free, dictatorship flourished.

I also grew up believing that countries where the press wasn't free were barbaric. Somehow I extended this logic to believe that the press would be independent and non-partisan in developed countries, where the press was free and you didn't usually hear of journalists getting arrested for writing stories the President didn't like. I thought it was in the enlightened self-interest of the press to be non-partisan. Coming to live in an enlightened society, I thought the press in America would not just be free, but without bias.

Enter Fox News.... I could not believe what I saw when I started watching Fox News in America. Their bias was 100%, complete and total. From Hannity to Cavuto, to Kelly, to the whole echelon of presenters and anchors, it was unbelievable. Their partisanship even affected the way they relayed regular news to the public. In America?

Fox News, though privately owned and funded, turned out to not be the independent, unbiased press organization I expected. To me, Fox News is the headquarters of the Publicity and Information Dissemination Office of the US Republican Party. To prove this point, they have had, as hosts, presenters, or regular commentators, well-known Republican faces like Sarah Palin, Karl Rove, Mike Huckabee, etc.

Watching MSNBC, you also see strong partisanship towards the Democratic Party, but you still get some CNN-style, non-partisan news and commentary in a broadcast. Fox news turned everything I believed about the press on its head, and here in a so-called civilized society. Remember, to me press freedom equaled independent, non-partisan press, which, in turn, equaled civilization, and civility.

I classify some sections of the American press TV as follows:

CNN –Independent news station, non-partisan, unparalleled worldwide reach, makes strong efforts to present the two sides of a political story. After watching a political news item on MSNBC or Fox News, you still need to watch CNN to remove the dross, and get the non-slanted story. However, CNN allows the overt support and lavish promotion of the gay agenda, mainly through its many self-professed gay anchors. These anchors deliberately go the extra mile to promote their own sexual orientation, rubbing the shine off the "independent" nature of the station.

MSNBC – Partisan, overtly against Republicans, promotes and supports abortion rights and the gay agenda, strongly supports President Obama and the Democratic Party.

Fox News – Partisan, Republican Party megaphone, supports US evangelicals and their anti-abortion agenda, overtly against President Obama and the Democratic Party. Fox News anchors really hate Barack Obama as President of the United States. I seriously believe that if anything bad should happen to that man, most people at Fox News would celebrate openly – even on prime time TV.

Chapter 7

Culture Shock

"So you have no credit in America –
no car loan, no mortgage, nothing?" The
way he said it, it was like having credit in
America is the qualification that would get
you into the kingdom of heaven.

7
Culture Shock

Speak Out, Loud and Clear

One of the things I have learned in America is to speak out. Americans deliver themselves with their mouths. If you gathered all the nationalities of the world together, the one that speaks with the loudest voice would be American. Growing up in Nigeria, when you spoke loudly, it was taken as a sign of arrogance and irreverence. We were taught to speak gently as a sign of modesty. Nigeria was a former British colony, and the Brits are very different from the Yankees.

In America, you have to speak out. Americans speak as if they want everyone to hear what they are saying. Whether at the Post Office, the mall, or on TV, even when having a simple conversation, Americans speak loudly. When you speak out, it is taken as a sign that you believe in yourself and have a strong conviction in what you are saying. When you speak quietly and not firmly, it is taken as a sign that you are not sure of what you are talking about, and in the work place, that is a sign of weakness.

I have worked with people who were not good at their job. Knowing their weakness, they made up for it by talking. They befriended the boss, and talked about their wives, their parents, their children's schools, a trip they took somewhere, and last weekend's game. They were often great conversationalists. The only thing they wouldn't talk much about was the job or how to solve a current problem!

I have learned that in America, you don't keep quiet. Americans talk. I have met people who spoke as if they owned heaven and earth, yet had little. I have known people who interviewed for a job they knew little about, yet came out of the interview ahead of those who were solid in the subject but who couldn't express themselves confidently. I think this is why the biggest and most daring con men are in America. I have seen people speak of a subject as if they were the ones who birthed the idea, even though they just read up on it online.

For example, I attended a training course some years back while preparing for my CISSP (Certified Information Systems Security Professional) tests. At one point, the instructor started talking about what is called "the Nigerian scam," which, in Nigeria (and elsewhere), is also known as "4-1-9." He described the crime and painted scenarios like he was there. What I found incredulous was when he started describing how government officials, from the President downward, participated in the crime, hosting the victims that were lured to Nigeria by criminals, how government officials, including Ministers (Secretaries), were maintaining lavish lifestyles from the proceeds of 4-1-9, and so on. He made it seem like the whole country was in on these crimes and that was what everyone lived on. The entire class was stupefied and were looking at him in awe – for having such detailed inside knowledge perhaps! When he finished, I raised my hand and informed the class that I came from Nigeria, and then gave them the information they really needed.

True, there is a crime called "4-1-9." It stems from someone writing you a letter or e-mail, giving you a too-good-to-be-true story as bait. For example, they could say there is money, maybe 100 million dollars, that belongs to your father or some other relative, and you just need 5,000 dollars to process it out of the bank. You know very well your Dad had never been to Nigeria, and had no business dealings with Nigeria, but you want to cash in on the non-existent millions. So, out of your greed, you part with 5,000 dollars, hoping to get the 100 million. What people don't know is that, in Nigeria, 5,000 dollars is a lot of money, currently about 800,000 Naira, Nigeria's local currency. For comparison, the MONTHLY pay for a chauffeur is about 30,000 Naira, about 200 dollars.

People fall for this scam because they think that coming out of Africa, the people there are likely to be stupid. They truly believe that the money is there, and the people soliciting them needed the "expertise" of a foreigner, probably a white foreigner, to get it out. This colonial mentality is the undoing of many who have fallen victim to the tricksters. As they say in Africa, "cunning man dies, cunning man buries him".

What the instructor didn't know is that government officials actually make efforts to round up and prosecute these tricksters, possibly under pressure from international trade partners like the United States and non-governmental agencies like Transparency International. He also didn't know, as we do, that Nigeria is an oil-rich country, able to make hundreds of millions of dollars daily when in full production. A lot of this oil money is said to be stolen. It is also common knowledge, both in Nigeria and outside, that there is corruption in Nigeria, inflation of contracts, etc. Government Ministers really have no time to lure people to Nigeria and deprive them of money. If they want to steal, these guys are administering millions of dollars and don't need a "measly" 5,000 dollars. I say this neither to support the evil of corruption, nor the other evil of "4-1-9", but just to point out the errors in that instructor's "eye-witness" account.

But I digress. The point is that Americans talk with such confidence that if you didn't have other facts, you would believe everything you hear. And Americans talk loud.

"Good morning"

Americans who travel to Africa are surprised at how many times a day they are greeted by the same person. It is customary to greet someone, or acknowledge them one way or another, no matter how many times you see them. People of my own cultural background of Western Nigeria greet people for almost everything under the sun. They greet you while standing (translates to something like "I greet you for standing"), or while sitting, or while on a journey, or while returning from one. They greet you for eating and for fasting, they greet you for sleeping and for waking up from sleep, and they greet you for working as well as for staying idle.

In fact, if you don't greet people in this way, you create the impression that you have a quarrel with them, or the relationship with them is strained.

Living in Philadelphia and Delaware showed me a big cultural difference – people don't greet each other much. People find it difficult to respond to "good morning." And if you say good morning to a colleague upon arriving at work, when you meet him a couple of hours later in the hallway, he doesn't expect you to greet him again.

Our first neighbor in Philadelphia wouldn't even acknowledge greetings. His daughters said "Hi" to my children a few times. While our standard greeting was "Good afternoon" (or morning or evening), we later realized that the standard American greeting is "Hi." My children adapted first, and my wife and I after many months. That still didn't stop me from greeting a colleague for a second or third time on the way to the coffee room.

When I raised this issue with a middle-aged white colleague at work he told me, "this is America – everyone minds their own business." He also told me if I was his neighbor and was greeting him every morning, he would wonder what was wrong with me!

I have since understood his views are not universal. I now understand that while such views may find a place in the north-east US, they don't in the South. In fact, in mannerisms, friendliness, and attitudes, people of the southern states: Georgia, Texas, Alabama, and others are nicer than the people of north-eastern US, They even say "Hi" or "How y'all doing?" before you even get a chance to greet them.

Then there is this "smile-flashing" which people do, especially in north-east US, probably in order to be polite. They see you, flash a smile which does not last a second, and their face goes back to normal. Whoever introduced this to corporate America may have robbed people of the joy of smiling a normal, regular smile. And if you are too busy, don't know the person, or don't feel comfortable enough to smile at them, then you are not obliged to smile. A smile is not a smile when it's not real.

Credit

In Africa, you are not expected to buy property, like a home or car, on credit. In America, the credit system is so well-entrenched that even if people have the cash, they think buying on credit is better.

In the initial days, I commuted between my apartment in the Philadelphia suburb of Cheltenham to City Line Avenue, my initial job posting. It was hard to take 2 different buses and the Septa train each way. After doing it for almost two months, I decided to approach a car dealership on the way home to try and buy a car. So I got down from the bus, armed with my letter of employment and pay stub, and confidently approached the dealership. They had a sign outside saying that your pay stub was all that was needed to buy a car. They gave me a form which I filled and I waited as the salesman keyed in some things on his computer.

"You have no credit," he blurted out.

I explained to him that I had just started work and showed him my pay stub. I told him how I had worked for about two months and needed a car because the weather was getting bad.

"Where were you working before then?"

"I was working in Africa."

"So you have no credit in America – no car loan, no mortgage, nothing?" The way he said it, it was like having credit in America is the qualification that would get you into the kingdom of heaven.

"No," I replied

"Then you can't buy a car. Nobody in America will sell you a car on credit."

He explained that the only way I could get a car would be if I paid in cash – to which I explained again that I had just started my job.

He became impatient with me and turned away to attend another customer. I was fortunate, a few weeks later, to buy a run-down Honda Accord car for $500 from a friend who was upgrading to a newer car – mind you, "newer" does not mean "new." The Honda had seen many previous owners, but still worked. At a monthly company social event following, I joked with my recruiter: "Jill, I bought a town-car." She was initially glad but soon exclaimed, with serious concern: "That must be expensive for you!" I explained that it was an old Honda Accord I could only use within town, not something I could travel with. She was relieved. She had thought I bought a Lincoln Town Car, a luxury sedan.

I have since realized that, while having good credit might not be the qualification for entering heaven, it serves you well here on earth in America, and it makes life much easier.

"Buying a House"

If you owned a house in Nigeria at the time I was coming to America, you owned every brick, nail and wood piece in it. You bought everything and paid for it fully, in cash.

At the time, most people built their homes themselves; so generally, you didn't buy or sell the home you had built! When you built a home, it was expected to pass from you to your children or relatives after your death. Even if you had built a rental property, you didn't sell it; your children were expected to take ownership of the property after you passed on. The only reason you sell your home would be if you ran into financial difficulties and your home had to be sold to pay creditors. This was rare and was considered a terrible failure. There were many idioms and proverbs that spoke negatively of someone who had to sell his house. It was a very bad thing to do.

In America, on the other hand, most people don't build their own homes, but buy them. After owning the home for some years, if you want, you could sell it and buy another one. It is very rare, for someone to build his own home from scratch, hiring all the labor and buying the materials to build it himself. So you buy a home that has been built by a company or a home someone else has lived in. No one ever thinks or says there is anything wrong with what the seller or the buyer does – it is the norm, the expected, the way things are done.

But you don't need to wait until you have all the money to pay for every brick in the home you are buying. With a good credit history and a small down-payment, you can take out a loan from a bank. Indeed you can buy a $200,000 house if you have a down-payment of as little as about $6,000+change. They usually spread the monthly payments over 30 years. In doing this, the house is held as security for the loan. If the owner does not pay, the bank is able to sell the house to recover its money.

So while owing some $194,000 out of $200,000, somehow you still get to call the house your own! As you continue to pay down the principal and interest, your equity in the home continues to increase until you pay it off. The bank protects itself in several ways. One way is that most of your monthly payments in the earlier years go to the interest, and very little goes to reducing the principal. At the end of the day, depending on the interest rate you get, you would have paid up to twice or 3 times the amount you borrowed before completing payments and owning the home 100%.

As I said earlier, mortgage loans are usually structured for a 30-year term, although shorter terms are possible. One thing I have observed is, whatever your age, they still give you a 30-year mortgage. So a 60-year old man would still get a 30-year mortgage. Come on, who are you kidding? Is someone saying the man is expected to be paying a mortgage when he is almost 90? What if he dies at 80 or 85? Wouldn't the bank lose money?

Well, we can safely say that no bank in America would lend a dime if they thought there was any chance they couldn't recover their money. The property is always held as collateral for the loan and the bank's investment is protected. The bank makes sure the house is insured against fire and other hazards. If the borrower cannot pay for the insurance, the bank contacts some insurance company and insures the property. Guess who pays for the insurance? The borrower! If the bank had refused a loan applicant because he was 60, he could sue them for discrimination based on age!

But when you really look at the financing arrangement, it helps people. Even young graduates have the opportunity to own their own beautiful homes without having all the money. Even if you had the cash, you might still take out a mortgage on the home you want to buy and invest the cash. This helps the economy to grow.

While the banks lend on the front end, there are back-end structures put in place by the government which guarantee the loans. One institution is Freddie Mac and the other is Fannie Mae. They make it possible for banks to lend on the front end, but they do not grant consumer loans themselves. So the government itself does not lend directly to individual citizens, as is done today in many African countries, including Nigeria.

However, there are a number of structures that make these arrangements work:

1.   First, every individual has to be uniquely identifiable in the system. This is afforded by the Social Security Number (SSN) or the Taxpayer's Identification Number (TIN).

2.   A credit-monitoring system has to be in place which monitors how faithfully a borrower pays his monthly bills. This assures the lender a person is a responsible borrower who has paid his bills in the past, and who is likely to be faithful in the future.

3.   Backing governmental financial institutions and structures like Freddie Mac and Fannie Mae which, at the backend, guarantee the loans and make it possible for banks to lend.

If African governments are able put these structures in place, their economies will surely be transformed.

All the ideas that make things work in America can be copied and adapted to local situations in other countries. America certainly does not have copyright on an idea, particularly ideas that work! The wheel can be adjusted to suit the vehicle, but there is no need to re-invent the wheel.

Chapter 8

Raising Children in America

It took us quite a while to understand that, in our absence, the American school system had re-oriented our children from what we taught them in Africa. The children did not come home to tell us of this corruption of our cultural values.

8
Raising Children in America

Look Up, Don't Look Down

When African children are disciplined, they are expected to listen attentively, looking down as they are scolded. You dare not stare back at your parents when they are correcting you. You are expected to respectfully look down or anywhere else but never at them. This was how my wife and I were raised in Africa, and this was how we started raising our own children.

After we got to America, unknown to us, one of the first things our children learned in school was to look straight at the person speaking to them, even when being disciplined. When they looked down or away, we later learned, it gave the person addressing them the impression they were lying or had something to hide.

It took us quite a while to understand that, in our absence, the American school system had re-oriented our children from what we taught them in Africa. The children did not come home to tell us of this corruption of our cultural values. The only way we knew was when there was an issue of discipline and they stared back at us in an "insulting" way (as we saw it) until we felt like dishing the child a dirty slap for this blatant "insolence."

One day we saw how another child was staring straight at his parents as they were correcting him. As my wife and I watched, amazed at the rudeness of the child, my older daughter used that occasion to explain to me what they had been taught in school. I confirmed this with a longer-term immigrant who helped re-orientate us. Since then, our children no longer look down or away when being disciplined. And I am sure anyone visiting us out of Africa or a JJC (JohnyJustCome) like we were, would still wonder at the "rudeness" of our children.

Have you greeted your elders?

I come from Western Nigeria, a place with very deep tradition and strong cultural values. Particular importance is attached to respect for one's elders. In my culture, boys and younger men are expected to prostrate when greeting elders – your parents, uncles, aunts, elderly neighbors, etc. Girls and younger women are expected to kneel down to greet older people. In fact, the wife is expected to greet her husband by kneeling and saying good things in his praise. This is still a tradition. Western education has eroded a lot of these values, but some still remain. For example, the modern wives still take the husband as the head of the home, but I don't think any still kneel down in the morning to greet their husbands – some of these couples were classmates in high school or college!

Coming to America, Western Nigerian families still teach their sons to prostrate when greeting elders, while the daughters are expected to kneel down. Children born in Africa understand this and do it to the best of their ability, while children born here try to do it but take it mostly as a joke. It is the pride of any family when, upon meeting older folks, their children prostrate properly or kneel down to greet them. It gives the parents a lot of joy because it sends the message they have trained their children properly. The person being greeted also feels a lot of joy because it shows the children accepted the training given them by their parents. As it is said where I grew up, it is one thing to train a child, it is a separate thing for the child to accept the training. So if, when meeting older people, your child has not greeted them properly, you hear things like "have you greeted your elders" or "is that how to prostrate?" (I must mention that even in Nigeria, prostrating and kneeling are peculiar only to the Yoruba people of Western Nigeria. There are other tribes in Nigeria where you stand to greet the elders, or you bow a little to show respect).

My wife and I went to our daughter's high school

prize-giving day the year she graduated. One of the students honored was a Nigerian student whose mother was a white American and whose father was a college professor from Western Nigeria. You would think that this woman would steer her children to fully imbibe American culture – but no, she loved Nigerian and African culture so much that she trained her children in Nigerian etiquette. .

That night, her son received many awards, and as the program was ending, all the graduating students were called up to the stage. They gave a final bow and started walking through the audience to exit at the back of the hall while we were clapping for them. As this young man was about to pass by where we were seated, he saw us and immediately stopped in his tracks. He fully prostrated before us and we were so glad that we reached out and congratulated him. We were so impressed. In our eyes, he was 10 feet tall! All the awards he had received were dwarfed by that singular act – that, among his mostly white colleagues, he displayed true fidelity to our culture without feeling ashamed about it. Since that day, as far as my wife and I are concerned, he can never do any wrong!

Spare the rod, spoil the child….

We learned soon after arriving America that you are not expected to spank your children when you discipline them. We were made to understand that when you beat a child, it is considered child abuse! I still don't know where that started, but many immigrant families have a problem embracing it.

Even the Bible tells us:

Foolishness is bound up in the heart of a child. The rod of correction will drive it far from him. (Proverbs 22:15 NKJV).

In more modern English, the passage is rendered as:

"A youngster's heart is filled with foolishness, but physical discipline will drive it far away" (Proverbs 22:15 NLT).

A similar passage says:

"Don't fail to discipline your children. They won't die if you spank them. Physical discipline may well save them from death" (Proverbs 23:13-14 NLT)

Not all parents agree that "Let's sit down and talk about it" is the right approach to correcting a child. There are times children will adamantly remain stubborn and want to continue doing a particular thing when parents have insisted they should not. The parent's remedy should not be "let's talk about it," because by that time, you have talked about it enough. A parent's next option is the "rod of correction." The law should not deprive parents of this opportunity to instill discipline into a child.

This was how our parents taught us, and we turned out well.

A Nigerian woman was trying to discipline her daughter and, in the process, beat her on the thigh with a coat-hanger.

The following day, the girl's teacher noticed the swelling and called the police. The end result: the woman, who was a nurse, lost her job! She couldn't get any other job until the incident was expunged from her record six months later.

Immigrant families, knowing what could get them into trouble with the law in America, have devised methods by which they discipline their children. As they say in Africa, if a child learns how to die, the mother learns how to bury the child. So they just follow some unwritten rules which are being written here for the first time. Just follow them in disciplining your child and you will be fine. It's a "How-To-Spank-Your-Child-Without-Getting-Into-Trouble-In-America" kind of guide.

1.   No matter what your child has done, control your anger, otherwise you will be forced to control it from inside a police cell.

2.   Don't spank your children in public. If someone saw you beating your child, or slapping him in public, they could call the police. They might truly perceive the boy is your son, but people make it their business to report everything they don't agree with.

3.   When you spank your child, make sure you don't leave any marks on their body, even if he had just broken the only family television while playing rough. You may spank them with material that will not leave a mark. Don't use a wire,

coat-hanger, or anything like that because these leave marks.

(Disclaimer: The reader is responsible for whatever results when spanking their child. This author will not be held liable in any way for any action of the reader).

4.   Don't beat your child on their bare skin – this is a sure way to leave a mark.

5.   Don't try to re-enact the beating you received from your parents on your child. That was then, this is now, and this is America. The goal should not be to spank to equate the child's error, but as a token of deterrence. So if for doing something bad when you were young, your parent gave you ten lashes, if you have to do it now, give your child just two or three.

6.   Speak again to your child after the spanking to let them know why you did it, Of course, you must have warned and explained many times earlier. If you explain well, they won't get you into the same position again. It becomes a partnership: you don't do that again, I won't do this again.

I told my children something like: "My father spanked me, but I never saw it as child abuse. I saw it as discipline. Your mom's father spanked her, but she saw it as discipline and not child abuse. If after I've died, you start saying your father abused you just because I beat you in disciplining you, I will wake up from my grave to haunt you!"

The Medicine Bottle

Saturday was our cleaning day. One Saturday, my wife entered our seventeen-year-old son's room. I don't know what she was looking for. After a few minutes in there, she burst out in anger: "Come and see what your son is doing! You are not watching over these children enough! I am doing the best I can with them, but you are not doing enough!"

I quickly rushed to her. "What is it? What happened?"

To which she replied: "Go and check your son's room!"

She had found a medicine bottle on which was written what she (and I) thought was the name of a popular drug which helps old and sexually weak men to become sexually stronger. I was devastated. I went in, saw the bottle by the bedside, and collapsed into the chair in the room.

I started thinking: "Oh my God! What is my son doing with this medicine? At his age? Where did I miss it? My wife was probably right – maybe I haven't been close enough to the children. Maybe I have put other things ahead of my parental duties. So my son is now sexually active. My God! We've taught him about abstinence, so how could this happen? So he probably has a girlfriend. Is she white or black? If black, is she an African-American, or an immigrant like us? But why would he be taking this medicine? He is supposed to be strong and able-bodied. I, his father, was strong in my younger days and remained strong today. Does he have a health issue he has not told us about?"

On and on I kept thinking. I picked up the bottle again. Yes, the label was clear enough: "ALLEGRA" it said.

"So how did my son get a hold of this performance-enhancing drug? But why would he be taking this at his age? What kind of a corrupting society have I brought my children into? Should we start thinking about going back home to raise our children? America has corrupted my son!"

My son came in a couple of hours later and you can bet we were prepared. He came upstairs, went into his room, and collapsed on the bed. My wife and I followed him less than a minute later. Seeing him collapsed on the bed bolstered in our minds the ready accusation we had for him.

"Where are you coming from?" I demanded.

"Work," he said simply. He continued, "I work Saturday mornings. I told you when I was leaving in the morning."

That was true, but didn't explain the evidence we had in our hands: the medicine bottle. So voila, I brought out the bottle.

"Whose is this?" I asked.

"Mine," he replied. Then the barrage of questions followed:

"What are you using it for?"

"Who prescribed it for you?"

"When did you start using it?"

His next answer terminated all the other questions in our mouths.

"My allergies," he said. Then it occurred to us... Wasn't there an ad on TV about a drug called Allegra for allergies, where they showed people enjoying the outdoors, in early spring?

Yes, Allegra - allergies. It made sense.

So how did we think we had come upon a bottle of VIAGRA in our son's room? We had never seen it before - it was later we learned it has a distinctive color!

Allegra – Viagra! Lord have mercy!

My wife and I, embarrassed to the bones, quickly apologized and crawled out of our son's room and back into ours. How stupid of us, I thought. Well, thank God we had realized our error before making too many accusations.

But then, looking at the brighter side: Thank God he wasn't on any performance-enhancing drug! He was still his father's son!

And there was no girl to worry about, yet, African or American!

Chapter 9

Shopping in America

When you say to a man: "Your Mama!" he wants to fight you. But when you say "Your Papa," he doesn't care – does he even know his (real) father?

9
Shopping in America

Every day in America, the stores gun for shoppers, or at least for their wallets, hoping they empty them on the goods and services in their store. They give lavish discounts and promotions, just hoping to attract you to step in. More often than not, having been drawn by the deep discount on a particular product, you are likely to buy more than you went in for once you entered the store: that's where they get you! So the most important thing to the retailer is to lure you in, sorry, to get you to step inside the store, by offering you sweet, tantalizing offers.

One of the ways retailers get you is offer you coupons. They send the coupons to your home by post, by e-mail, or even your cell phone. If that's not enough, they also give you coupons at the checkout counter as you pay for a purchase. The coupon could offer you a discount on a specific item, or on several items in the store. That coupon will be valid next time you go into the store, not on anything you've already bought that day, ensuring that you come back soon. I got a coupon recently, when I went for Labor Day shopping. Printed along with my receipt was a coupon that said:

BONUS CA$H

$30.00 OFF

Congratulations!! You've just earned XYZ BONUS CA$H, redeemable on apparel, shoes, accessories, jewelries, or home merchandise.

Valid: Tuesday thru Wednesday.

Redeemable on your next qualifying purchases, excluding taxes. Does not apply to Doorbusters, Big Buys, Best Value, Levis, Disney Shop, Assets Red Hat, Label by Spanx, Licensed Team Sports Merchandise, Nike, Clarks, Athletic Shoes, Jewelry, Trunk Shows, the Diamond Vault, TechnoMarine Watches, Sephora, La Dreuset, Sophie Conran, Royal Doulton, Celebrations, Food, Kitchen Electrics, Floor Care, Joseph Joseph, Hunter Douglas, In-home Custom Decorating, Fitness Equipment and Accessories, Art. com, Baby Gear, Personalized Jewelry, Services, Service Plans, Gift Cards, Closing Store Purchases, current orders and prior purchases, or in combination with other coupon(s). No cash value.

VALID IN STORE ONLY.

What is remarkable about this coupon is not what you can buy with it, but what you can't buy with it! By the time you exclude all the items it is not applicable for, the immigrant in me cries out: WHAT'S LEFT?? And even then, it is only valid for your next qualifying purchases and cannot be combined with any other coupon and is valid on ONLY two specific days and only in apparel, shoes, accessories, jewelries, or home merchandise! I ask again: WHAT'S LEFT?? So the coupon, though it seems attractive, is targeted, and narrowed down, and so restricted that you can only benefit from it when you buy a few specific things. Behind the scenes, the computer checkout program would have been coded to obey all the restrictions and exclusions. Truly, there is no free money in America!

The so-called holiday shopping season starts with Thanksgiving in November. Thanksgiving is celebrated on the fourth Thursday of November every year and is America's biggest holiday. Wherever you are, you connect with family and friends at Thanksgiving and share Thanksgiving dinner together.

The shopping for the Thanksgiving dinner itself is quite small compared to what happens the day after. The day after Thanksgiving is Black Friday, when the stores offer unbelievable discounts on many products, and sell many other products at prices far below normal. They also open early on Black Friday, as early as 4am. As a result, shoppers go and line up overnight to make sure they get the items they want.

At our first attempt at Black Friday (we were trying to get a computer advertised for $250, less than half the normal price)we got to the stores at 8am and learned that all the deeply discounted products had been bought. So we went home, disappointed. The following year, we went earlier, but not as early as the first set of people in line. This time, we were able to get the trick behind the Black Friday

You see, there may be only 3 units of the hugely discounted and widely advertised computer (or TV, or stereo) in the entire store. Once those are bought by the people who got there first, you are left with the rest of the stock at regular prices, which, even if they carry discounts, might not make a penny-watching immigrant to jump in and buy. So, for the second year running, we could not buy any of the "star" advertised products. In order not to make the trip a total waste, we decided to buy some clothes for our children who had made the early morning trip with us. But this is why the stores do such things. We were not there to buy clothes in the first place! So they successfully lured us in, sold us something we weren't shopping for, and still got our money one way or the other. People continue to flood the stores every year for Black Friday shopping, and as they say here in America, a sucker is born every day! In recent times, greedy stores have been starting Black Friday on Thanksgiving Day, which some believe is desecrating the family-togetherness of the holiday.

You would think, with the money they made on Black Friday, retailers would be satisfied, but no! They now have Cyber Monday, online shopping on the Monday following Black Friday. Cyber Monday has been encouraged by the fact that internet shopping has come to stay. Most errands for which you need to get out of your home or office can now be done online. On Cyber Monday, people flood the internet to shop and I believe that very soon, Cyber Monday sales will dwarf the Black Friday in-store sales.

Christmas comes but once a year, as the saying goes, and American retailers make full use of it. Advertisements for Christmas shopping start rolling out right after Thanksgiving and sometimes even before.

Every business tries to take advantage of the shopping at Christmas, especially with the tradition of gift-giving. This tradition is entrenched in the fabric of American society. So for the Christmas shopping season, starting in late November, America becomes the target of stores and businesses. Stores are lavishly decorated in the Christmas theme, discount coupons are issued to frequent shoppers, extra hands are hired by retailers, shopping hours are extended, and several promotions are organized by different stores just to lure shoppers. It's a huge, huge operation. The TV and radio stations assail consumers with advertisements tailor-made for the holiday. Even car companies advertise their vehicles as possible gifts. .Shoppers flood the stores from morning till night.

I must briefly mention here a trend that started soon after we arrived in America. It is becoming a custom for some establishments, even government agencies, to not mention the word "Christmas," because it contains the word "Christ." In order for the speaker can remain religiously neutral, store clerks, teachers, government officials etc do not use the word "Christmas" because it might be offensive to some people. So instead of people saying the good old "Merry Christmas" to you, they say "Happy Holidays." And instead of the stores advertising for "Christmas Shopping," they advertise "Holiday Shopping."

To those of us who grew up as Christians, before coming to live in a society doing everything possible to become God-less, it all seems so childish. This year is actually called 2014 A.D., and you know what that means? 2014 Anno Dominis: "In the year of the Lord," and "the Lord" being referred to is Jesus Christ!

More so, December 25 will always be "Christmas Day," it will never be called "Holiday Day," and there is nothing anyone can do about that. One thing I do though, I loudly reply "Merry Christmas" even if greeted with "Happy Holidays."

By the time Christmas comes and goes on December 25, New Year's shopping begins. Advertisements still continue to flood the airwaves, this time for New Years shopping. Shops aim to drain consumers of whatever they didn't spend at Christmas.

And right after New Year, retailers re-decorate their stores for President's Day sales. Presidents Day (also known as Washington's Birthday) is a federal holiday held on the third Monday of February. The day honors presidents of the United States, including George Washington, the first president of the United States.

After President's Day, they re-decorate their stores for the Valentine's Day sales. Valentine's Day is on February 14 and celebrates lovers and the expression of love. It is celebrated lavishly with pink and red hearts, roses, cupids, and other representations of love. Most stores are decorated with these themes and give out special discounts in honor of the holiday. This holiday seems to touch everyone because most people have special people in their lives –husbands and wives, boyfriends and girlfriends.

After Valentine Day goes, there comes spring, spring break, and March Madness……. Retailers theme their sales and offers after any of these events.

When the March Madness goes, there comes Easter, and with it comes another opportunity to lure shoppers into the stores.

When Easter goes, retailers re-decorate their stores and put out advertisements for Mother's Day. Mother's day comes on the second Sunday in May and is widely celebrated all over the United States, more than Father's Day. The way shoppers are bombarded with advertisements proves this.

I really think that it makes sense for Mother's Day to be celebrated more than Father's Day. First, we often hear of disputes over the father of a child (hence the need for paternity tests and paternity suits), but there is hardly ever a doubt over the mother. In addition, the unique role of the mother in the life of a child makes many want to fight you if you say anything negative about their mothers. When you say to a man: "Your Mama!" he wants to fight you. But when you say "Your Papa," he doesn't care – does he even know his (real) father? Also, it is the father who usually walks away from a marriage – leaving the children with the mother.

When Mother's Day shopping is done, the stores re-decorate again for Memorial Day. Memorial Day is a federal holiday on the last Monday of May to honor all those who died while serving in the military, and traditionally marks the start of the summer season.

Not to be outdone, fathers are honored on Father's Day on the third Sunday of June, with the stores luring shoppers again with advertisements and promotions.

July 4 is Independence Day, to mark the declaration of independence of the US from Britain in 1776. If the day were not continuously celebrated, it would be hard to believe this country was ever under any foreign rule, ever. While the day is marked with parades in many cities, they also have fireworks displays in the evenings. Of course, stores begin advertising for special sales way ahead of time and decorate in US flags and national colors of blue, red and white.

Labor Day is observed on the first Monday in September and traditionally marks the end of summer. Of course, it is given its own share of attention by the stores.

Halloween is celebrated on the 31st of October. It is said that Halloween originated from the Church and was meant to celebrate departed saints of the Church. In Halloween celebrations today, however, there is hardly anything "churchy" about it. Rather, the Halloween we see in America today celebrates witchcraft, horror, death, and all sorts of evil. Many churches, ours included, celebrate Halleluyah Night instead of Halloween, in order to prevent children from getting involved in all the evil Halloween symbolizes. In these churches, Halleluyah Night is an evening of games, parties, and eating.

Other holidays and special days around which stores and businesses advertise their products are:

- Martin Luther King Day, (third Monday of January);

- Lincoln's Birthday, (on February 12);

- St. Patrick's Day, an Irish religious holiday, on March 17. St Patrick's Day is celebrated by many, even those who don't know where Ireland is;

- Columbus Day, (the second Monday in October); and

- Veterans' Day (on November 11).

The bottom line is that whatever the holiday, the goal of the stores is to find a way to get you to stop by. Once you are in, you are not likely to buy only the things you went to the stores for.

While America pays good money to skilled and experienced people, they have also opened up opportunities for where this money will go. It is a way that makes the money go round, and everyone benefits in some way at the end.

No matter how smart you think you are, you will part with your money in America.

Chapter 10

Sports in America

It may not be a bad idea to rename the NFL (National Football
League) as the NH&RL (National
Handball and Running League) –
because that is what it is!

10
Sports in America

S ports, in America, are not just a pastime, but a pillar of the national economy. Many celebrities and million-aires in America today became famous and/or made their money through sports. Whatever the size of the game ball, egg-sized like a golf ball, lime-sized like a tennis ball, orange-sized like a baseball, oval like an American football, or watermelon-sized like a basketball, soccer ball, or volleyball, people have made millions of dollars kicking, throwing, batting and hitting them. Even when there is no ball in a sport, people still make millions, year in and year out - whether running, swimming, walking, rowing, jumping, horse-riding, car-racing, you name it.

As players have made millions, so coaches and trainers have made millions. And, of course, all these sports have to be broadcast on radio and television and reported in newspapers and online, so reporters and TV crews make good money, too. And the sporting facilities: golf courses, stadiums, basketball courts, gyms, tennis courts, etc have to be maintained year-round, so maintenance crews make money. In accommodating players, fans, and reporters, hotels make money too. Advertisers and the sports marketing companies also make huge money from sports.

From what I have seen in America, it makes sense for the national economy that 300 million people would not just follow one sport, but many. Generally, the sports calendar is planned so one sport does not get in the way of another. So all year round, there is something going on. Each sport is generously reported and documented by the press. Large news organizations don't just have sports reporters, but tennis reporters, basketball reporters, etc. Coming from a background where emphasis is on one sport, soccer, I seriously feel my native country and many other nations shortchange themselves by not deliberately promoting other sports, as America does.

In America, many sports programs are available, from elementary through high school and into college. High school sportsmen become college sportsmen, and college sportsmen become professional players. It is a natural progression. Coaches and facilities are available even at elementary schools, and the school curriculum allows sports as a part of education. There are also championships at all levels of education, with awards and medals that encourage student participation.

Soccer - Never #1

Soccer is the beloved national sport of most countries, but from what I have seen in the USA, it is unlikely to ever become the most popular sport in America. True, millions of people now watch soccer, and Major League Soccer (MLS) is quite active, yet news of soccer hardly enters mainstream sports reporting in the US.

You see, Americans grew up seeing soccer not as a mainstream American sport, an idea that passes down generations. Another reason is there is too much money being made by those controlling professional sports in America. The NFL, which controls Football, is said to be a $32 billion business. It is natural that the American sports will always get wider exposure in the USA than soccer.

Despite all these, the popularity of soccer in the U.S. has been growing, and soccer is the third most played team sport in the U.S., bested only by basketball and baseball. It can be safely predicted these popular US sports would soon be overrun by the popularity of soccer, should it get as much press coverage and TV airtime as say, baseball, in the course of a normal daily life.

"Organized Violence"

I understand American football to a great extent, and I think it is an exciting sport, requiring physically fit and intelligent players. You have to be strong in your bones and muscles to survive five 300-pound men jumping on top of you! Due to its roughness, my wife calls the sport "organized violence."

I still don't understand why they call this sport "football." The only time you use the foot to kick the ball is when a team fails to advance the ball 10 yards after three attempts or at the start of a turn. For the rest of the game, the ball is thrown. So essentially, American "football" is purely handball and a lot of running! That is not what the rest of the world calls football. What the world knows as football is what America calls soccer, and it is the most popular sport in the world. It may not be a bad idea to rename the NFL (National Football League) as the NH&RL (National Handball and Running League) – because that is what it is!

But what I like about American football is the glamour and pomp that surrounds it. You can see this at any of the games, especially at the national finals, which is called the Super Bowl. In my view, the Super Bowl is the most glamorous finals of any sport on the surface of the earth, and it gets better every year. Just like they do in baseball, Americans also call the winners of the Super Bowl "World Champions".

Someone told me soon after I arrived in America that, in the past, black players were never selected to be quarterbacks at all levels of the game, from high school football, to college football, and to NFL teams. As I was told, the white coaches believed that black players did not have as much intelligence as white players and couldn't play the quarterback position, which requires fast and intelligent thinking.

Well, I don't know how true this was in the past, but

a year after we arrived the US, Donovan McNabb, a black player, was starting quarterback for the Philadelphia Eagles (our team in the Greater Philadelphia area). McNabb led the Eagles to four consecutive NFC East Division Championships in 2001, 2002, 2003, and 2004, as well as Super Bowl 39 in February 2005. McNabb was a smart and intelligent player, but he made some unserious plays, which made me mad because it could give credence in some bigoted minds to the old-time idea about black players not being capable quarterbacks (if that idea was ever true).

People like McNabb should always know that, in every case where there has been historically bigoted opinions and judgments about their race, they represent not only themselves, but all the people of their race. They need to give the best performances of their lives every time to shut the mouths of bigots. They need to always aim to obtain results that terminate insults. Jesse Owens did this at the 1936 Summer Olympics in Berlin, Germany, and according to Wikipedia, was "credited with single-handedly crushing Hitler's myth of Aryan supremacy".

In any case, in today's world, not only are there black quarterbacks, but there are very successful black coaches who have reached, and won, the Super Bowl.

There was a time it was believed that the earth was flat, until it was proven the earth is round. It must have taken some people in those generations some time to come to accept the fact we take for granted today. The fact that the world has changed or is changing does not wipe out the fact of the bigotry of the past. It might still take some people time to realize that a new day has already dawned in America, and that every human being in this country is now considered a whole person.

So there are still bigots in America, who still hold onto the backward views of the past. No one can do anything about that. You can't wash it out of them. The only thing the McNabbs of America can do is to continually do their best to excel. They must take every game seriously and do the very best they can. The good thing is the bigots will always be in the small minority, and the last time I checked, the majority still rules.

"World" Championship Series

I've spent 15 years in America, and I still don't understand how baseball is played. The only thing I know about baseball is when the ball is batted out of the field, it is a home run. I have been to a number of baseball games, mostly sponsored by the companies I worked for. Baseball is a US national pastime.

From what I've seen, people go to a baseball game for more than the game itself. It is a time to relax, eat snacks, and have a few drinks in the open with thousands of people doing the same around you. It's a game to take children to, a sport which helps friends and families bond. The tense, nail-biting, heartbeat-pounding nature of soccer (which could last from the start of a game until the final whistle), is not there. Understand me, baseball has a lot of its own excitement, otherwise people wouldn't be buying season tickets or going to watch all year round without missing a game.

It is funny that when teams within the USA play against each other in the baseball championships they call it the World Series – but it's only America! I wish they knew what goes into becoming the winner of the World Soccer Cup (or the World Cup, as it is known outside of the USA). That is the real World Series, the real World Cup. In all honesty, calling the US Major League Baseball championship the "World Series" is nothing short of self aggrandizement.

The Sun Never Sets

If you are good at sports and live a responsible and decent life, the sun will never set for you financially in America. In your playing days, you make a lot of money because American professional sportsmen and women get a lot of money through salaries, endorsements, and sponsorships.

You see, America celebrates success. So product marketers want admirable sportsmen to identify with their product, even if they don't use the product. It's a win-win situation. The sportsmen make money, and the products and their manufacturer get the exposure they need.

When an athlete's playing days are over, they continue to make money through advertisements, as well as sports analysis for TV and Radio stations, appearances and speeches. The bigger a star they were and the more scandal-free life they lived, the bigger the contracts. It is reported that Michael Jordan, the great Basketball star made $90 million in 2013, most of it from endorsements. That is higher income than was made by any current player in basketball, football, baseball, or soccer!

Many sports people make good money and invest it wisely, while some fritter their good fortune away, becoming paupers at the end of the day, poorer than those who never threw or caught a ball.

The Sports Engine

In my view, sports journalists have contributed the most to the widespread attention given to sports in America. They really are the engine on which sports run. I love the way they reel out the statistics of every sport: "the shot was the fastest in the league since 2005," "the most rebounds in the 4th quarter since Kobe Bryant 10 years ago," "the most points the Eagles have scored at home against Green Bay Packers in 15 years," and so on. This, of course, must be backed by a lot of research in the days leading to the game. Sports journalists are people who love the sport itself and understand it very well, and not just pool reporters.

Before the game, sports journalists target the players for interviews: "what was going on in your mind when you took that shot" kind of interview. They stalk the players and their families for photographs and stories, camp in their neighborhoods, etc. Sports journalists make heroes and gods out of players, thereby challenging them to live up to the billing. And while the game is on, having done their research and interviews, they tell you stories about the player, his wife or girlfriend, his son or daughter, his brother or sister, his fears, his strengths, his weaknesses, generally making them humans, at the same time they are making them gods.

And because there are so many news outlets, there are thousands of reporters who want to chronicle every little detail about a player's younger days or family background for the rest of us. This challenges sportsmen and women to greater performances.

The demand for greater performance creates a real challenge for those who do not posses natural talents or who have reached their limit. In order to maintain the superstar image, some sportsmen resort to drugs and other performance-enhancement methods. And guess who would also probe them and hound them down for the juicy story? Yes, you guessed right: sports journalists!

"I love this game"

In my opinion, basketball is the Cinderella of American sports. This is a sport where the transition from a high school player to a professional is probably the easiest, and several players have done it successfully. Basketball is different because all that is needed to play is a hoop and net. You can set up basketball practice in the back yard, in the driveway, and against the garage wall.

I also believe that the NBA and their marketers are the most creative of all the sports leagues. They make you love the game. With the generous use of sight and sound, and a championship which, due to its length, was designed to catch your attention, you will eventually hear of the championship series, even if you are not a basketball fan.

Chapter 11

African Immigrants in America

When most people come to America, they get another degree called B.A., meaning Begin Again! Whatever your original qualification, more often than not, you have to train for something different, something that has strong employment potentials.

11
African Immigrants in America

Gone are the days when all the Nigerians symbolized in America was a chain of drug couriers arrested at US airports or credit card fraudsters. The Nigerian in America, and indeed, the African immigrant in America today has come a long way from those shameful days. The typical African immigrant is most likely a professional. They abound as information technology specialists, doctors, nurses, pharmacists, sportsmen, university lecturers, etc. Granted, like in every human group, there are a few bad eggs who want to get rich without working for it, but this is not the case with most African immigrants in America.

Begin Again

When most people come to America, they get another degree called B.A., meaning Begin Again! Whatever your original qualification, more often than not, you have to train for something different, something that has strong employment potentials. And more often than not, you have to start with a lowly job, which might be far below your skills and ability. You may start as a security guard or as a Certified Nursing Assistant (CNA). You might work in a parking garage or as a store clerk. While at this lowly job, you may start on a degree course, or study for tests which allow you to convert your professional license from Africa to the American version. Medical doctors, nurses, pharmacists, and lawyers have to do a series of tests in order to be able to work in their professional fields in the US, no matter the level of experience they had back home.

The only professionals who might be able to work right away without these conversion tests are probably computer and information technology professionals, as well as university lecturers. The computers and software which IT professionals trained and worked on in their homelands were made in America in the first place, and, given the right level of experience, the transition is often smooth. In technology, you either know it or you don't, and if you can prove to an employer that you have the knowledge, skills, and experience, you can get on the job. As for college professors, their reputation often precedes them, as the journals they publish in are international, and their knowledge is easily verified by the university or college hiring them.

For many others, while they are working as security guards, they are studying to obtain a college degree. While working as a CNA, they are studying to become a Licensed Practical Nurse (LPN). And after they get the LPN, they aspire to become a Registered Nurse (RN). You would think they would stop there, but they often don't. In a few years they get a Bachelor's degree in Nursing, while many go on to get a Master's degree. I have seen some who, after stabilizing their families with income from a nursing qualification, proceed to medical schools and are today working as medical doctors in America. If it is professional training for which there is a certification which could advance his career, the African immigrant will work hard to get it.

The average Nigerian in America is here for the long haul. Even if the economic and electrical power situation improves back in Nigeria, there is not likely to be a mass exodus out of the US. In their later years, however, some are more likely to return to a Nigeria that boasts good electricity, while others will continue in America until they reach retirement. They are likely to follow the Nigerian saying: you come home to rest after a day of hard work at the farm.

Most people would not want to end up in Nursing Homes in the old ages, if their children become too Americanized to take care of them. And most people also do not want to be driving themselves around at the age of eighty, as some elderly Americans do today. There is plenty of cheap help in Africa, and this might be the main reason elderly Africans would retire back to their home countries.

The Hardship Factor

The class of Africans the American society needs to watch out for are those who are schooling or have schooled in America, especially those brought to America after they became knowledgeable about their environment in Africa. I do not have the statistics, but I would bet if you examined high school results and college admissions in the last 10 to 15 years, children of Nigerian parentage or origin have excelled in disproportionate high numbers. These children may be listed in the census data today as American citizens, but I am speaking of parental or family origin, even if the parent is now a naturalized American citizen.

There is something in the Nigerian that pushes him higher, to want to do more than is required of him to do. From my own perspective, it is the "hardship" factor. Most of us who came in as adults studied for our School Certificate examinations (SATs) with candlelight and lamps, as most students in Nigeria still do today. Transportation was hard for us. There were no school buses and there are still none today. Drinkable water did not flow from our taps and still doesn't flow in most homes in Nigeria. Our toilets in high school were not the water closet system.

We were toughened from childhood by sickness (particularly malaria, which you get many times over in the course of a lifetime) and we remained sick for days in poor and expensive medical facilities. When we went to college in Nigeria, almost 10 of us slept on three bunk beds in a room no bigger than my daughter's dorm room in America. With the hard lives we lived at young ages (which American children cannot imagine), the average African immigrant is still able to compete in the job place and stand shoulder to shoulder with colleagues who did not have such hardships.

Also, in the Nigeria I grew up in, a good education catapulted you into the middle class. So even very poor parents sold all they had to get their children a good education. It was only through education you could stand with the children of the rich and the privileged, and Nigerians took it very seriously.

My wife tells her colleagues in the office: "I can't misbehave or mess up with my work because I have come 6,000 miles from home to get here." As an immigrant, you have so much to lose if you are caught on the wrong side of the fence. Sensible immigrants work hard, play by the rules, and are risk-averse.

Living in Africa in America

As an African immigrant, food could send you scurrying back to your native country. Not the lack, but the availability of the type of food you were used to eating back home.

Earlier African immigrants might have faced this problem, but not us 21st century immigrants. Every large city has at least one "African Market" or "African Store." In such a place, you can get African staple food and meats of all varieties. Almost everything is there. Even the kind of cocoa people drink back home (Bournvita and Milo) is there. There is hardly anything you want to buy as an African that you can't get in an African store in America. In fact, we boast to people back in Africa: for food, we don't miss home!

African immigrants do two sets of grocery shopping. One is the standard grocery shopping in the standard grocery stores (Acme, Superfresh, Shoprite, Publix, etc), while the other is the African Store shopping. You can't get everything in the African Store. They don't carry Bounty paper towels, toilet tissue, American bath soap (although they carry some African ones), ice cream, etc. But the standard stores also don't carry foofoo flour, yam flour, cassava flour, tripe (intestine of cow), cow leg, goat meat, dried fish, etc.

So you do your standard grocery shopping, for the children and the home, in the standard grocery store (in our case, it's Acme or Shoprite, both are close to our home). Then you head to the African Store for the second set of grocery shopping. The biggest benefit of the African store is African food, and some of the children prefer the African food, while most prefer standard American food. So, down the line, there will be something in your grocery shopping for everybody.

My children all know how to make African food, and when my son was younger, he would actually cry if his older sister failed to give him a portion of the Amala (yam flour porridge) she made. They also know a lot about the American food culture and restaurants, more than my wife and I! I believe they are having the best of both worlds.

There are bulk purchase places that cater to the African taste. If you were buying goat meat, for example, in some quantity, you could buy it directly from the meat farm, and it comes a lot cheaper. A couple of families could band together to share a goat.

There are also a number of African restaurants, especially in the larger cities – Philadelphia, New York, Chicago, and Atlanta, for example. At those in Philadelphia, I have seen a few Americans come in to eat the foofoo and other African foods. Hopefully, in the next few years, these restaurants will increase in number and regular restaurants will begin to offer some African fare.

It is all like living in Africa in America.

The Hour of Segregation

11am Sunday morning is said to be the most segregated hour in America. At this time, most churches are holding Sunday services. Whites attend predominantly white churches, blacks attend predominantly black churches, Koreans attend predominantly Korean churches, and yes, Africans attend predominantly African churches, at more nationalistic levels.

There are branches of churches started in Nigeria, churches started in Ghana, Kenya, etc. So in Nigeria-originated churches, Nigerians are an absolute majority, if not the entire population. The situation is similar for Ghana-originated churches, Kenya-originated churches, etc. Those churches still practice the doctrines of the mother church back home in Africa, and the dressing and songs are colorful and cultural. You see, the members were probably members, elders and Pastors in the mother church back in Africa before they came to settle in the US. Others were members of like-minded churches as the mother-church in Africa.

The only difference is that each Church has to be registered at the state level, mainly as a not-for-profit organization. Each church also registers with the dreaded US Internal Revenue Service (IRS). You can joke with every other thing in America, but you can't joke with the IRS. While there may be little regulation of churches back in Africa, in America, the fear of the IRS is the beginning of a Pastor's wisdom. But, for people who follow the guidelines, there is really nothing to fear.

Apart from registering with the relevant authorities, when renting a building for church or building your own, you have to seek the approval of the Planning and Zoning department of the County (or City or Town). The place must have been zoned in the area's master plan as a possible location for a church. There are many other requirements, part of which is the number of parking spaces you must have. If you are in the suburbs, you cannot plan to park on the road. In Delaware, where we are located, you have to have at least one parking space for every four proposed worshippers. So a church of 100 people must have at least 25 parking spaces.

The Department of Transportation also has to approve your plans, to be sure vehicles can enter and leave the premises without blocking road traffic. The Fire Marshall also has to approve your plans, to be sure, in case of a fire, there is space for the Fire Engine to enter the premises, there is water cistern nearby, emergency exits are available and are not blocked and the exit points inside the building can be easily found. Before you move in, all these Departments have to come and inspect everything to be sure the building is in full compliance before you can get a certificate of occupancy, without which you cannot move in.

While these steps may look laborious and difficult, if you really look into them, they are meant to preserve human life. Americans plan ahead. (I have seen many churches started under tents in Nigeria, and, while still holding services under the tent, a whole building is built around the tent until it is roofed, and the arrival of the church building is celebrated, even when the walls have not been plastered nor painted, when there is no water in the building, when toilets don't yet function, etc).

So, as for Church, you go to a Church where the congregation is primarily from Africa, and it's like living in Africa while in America.

African parties are always fun, and whether it is summer or winter, Africans throw parties. It could be for a wedding, a birthday, a baby naming ceremony, a house-warming or some other event. Of course, there is a lot of African food.

The only thing we don't do as they do back home is funerals. The funeral homes don't dance, play band trumpets or drums, and they don't throw the casket up and down in dancing (an act which always comes with the possibility of the body in it being disheveled from so much throwing up and down). Back home, from the point they start dancing with the casket, up till interment, no one opens the casket. I wish families would begin to do this: view whatever is left of the body in the casket after all the dancing is done.

Consistency of Africa

There is a consistency about Africa that Africans themselves take for granted, but which, when you start sojourning abroad, stares you right in the face. In Africa, you don't need special clothes for special seasons. The shirt or dress you wore in the rainy season you can wear in the dry season. However, in the US and Western world, God save you if you don't buy new clothes at the beginning of a season or dig out last season's clothes.

Winter is the only time African immigrants admit they miss their land. You often hear Africans saying: "God blessed our land. If it was home, it would never be as cold as this." The weather in Africa is fairly consistent. When it is hot, it is hot, but not burning hot, and when it is cold, it is never freezing. In America, you deal with spring, summer, fall and winter, each season requiring different clothes than the last.

In Africa, some people make plans to travel abroad without thinking of the weather overseas, and believe me the weather could make your arrival a nightmare. If you arrived in winter, you could even face problems at the airport, as your plane may not be able to land due to bad weather. A winter storm could keep everyone off the streets, including people who were scheduled to pick you up at the airport. In Africa, oh blessed Africa! Nothing like that: you breeze in and out 365 days a year. Same clothes, all seasons!

If you arrived the US in winter, your hosts are likely to meet you at the airport with warm jackets, if they are kind enough, otherwise you have to get one within a few hours if you don't want to freeze to death. Your hands get numb by the biting cold, and your face is frosted. No matter how warm you dress, the cold still finds a way to parts of your body. If, for any reason, the home of your host is not well heated, you could be freezing all through the night. This usually happens if they maintain rigid thermostat control in order to limit the heating bills, which can get very expensive. I have heard new immigrants and visitors complain that the home of their hosts was not well heated. Well, they don't realize what it costs to keep the house heated.

I have seen struggling immigrant families turn off the heat even in winter and resort to covering up with blankets and comforters as they move about the home. Living in America can be hard if you don't have money for the basic essentials! Those who know about a struggling family often lend a hand, and they can also get help from their church community. But other immigrants can only stretch themselves so far, because they too, are just one paycheck away from losing some essential comfort. These struggles are especially common in the earlier days of settling in America. These cases have other immigrants saying: "Why doesn't he go back home? You shouldn't leave the comfort of Africa to come and die in America!" They conveniently forget the comfort we are talking about goes beyond the weather, and extends to jobs, security, peace of mind, good hospitals, etc.

Your house is not the only thing you have to heat; your car's heating system should be working in winter, too. You might not have heat in your car if you could only afford an older car, which you are likely to do as a new immigrant or if you are a student. Getting a car with working heat is not a luxury, nor a wasteful expense, but sheer necessity. I've seen students who drive year after year in cars with broken heating systems. They wear gloves and thick socks, and even blankets in the car. It is just not the best place to be. Thank God those students are well settled now!

While the cold of winter is tough, the heat of summer is also unbearable. Just as you have to have your home and car heated in the winter, you also need air conditioning in your home and car in summer. Having lived in Lagos, Nigeria, most of my life before coming to America, I could never have imagined there was a place in this world hotter than Lagos. You see, the weather is hot and humid in Lagos, but we didn't know that and never talked of it. In the US however, even total strangers come up to you to say, "it's darn too hot and humid today," as if it's a ravaging plague or a national calamity! Come on, I lived in this stuff for decades and I didn't die. Nobody ever came up to me in Lagos to say how humid it is: "hot" and "humid" just equals "hot." When it is hot in America, all the experiences you had living in the hot weather of Nigeria becomes child's play, and I'm just talking of Delaware/ Pennsylvania weather, not even Arizona or Nevada!

Then there is the consistency of daylight in Africa. When light shines in through your window in Nigeria, you know it is after 6 am, and when it starts to get dark, you know it's probably after 7 pm. This is generally consistent all the year round. Not so in America. When winter is near, it gets dark by about 5 pm and daylight comes at about 7 am. When spring is going and summer is approaching, daylight comes about 5 am, and it will still be bright outside at 9 pm. In the height of summer, at 9 pm, you can still see clearly outside:

longer days and shorter nights. In Africa, if it's bright and clear outside at 9 pm or starts getting dark by 4:30 pm, people would think the end of the world had come. Some would pray and some would consult their gods.

Chapter 12

Why Things Work in America

With what I have seen in America, any nation that does not implement a unique, mandatory National Identification numbering system is hugely short-changing itself, its people, and its economy.

12
Why Things Work in America

A Unique National Identification Number

The primary thing which makes things work in America is the fact that there is no anonymity in the system: every resident or citizen is identifiable throughout the system, through the use of a unique Social Security Number, or SSN. This number is unique to you, and if you were born in America, is given to you as soon as your parents are able to apply for it. All that is required is your birth certificate. If you are an immigrant, you can get a SSN through your immigration status and entry into the United States. The SSN is required by your employer before they can put you on payroll. It is required by the State licensing office before they issue you a Driver's License or State ID. It is required if you are opening a bank account, if you are renting or buying a home, and when filing your taxes.

The SSN identifies you through the system. While police

will only request your Driver's license when they stop you for a traffic violation, the Driver's license itself is tied to your SSN, and the police have direct access to the State's licenses database. In addition, your car registration is tied to your Driver's license, which, as we have said, is also tied to your SSN. This has made it easy for the authorities to install and operate unmanned traffic enforcement camera system. If you run the red light, a camera automatically takes a picture of your vehicle and a couple of weeks later you get a traffic violation ticket in the mail. You cannot commit a crime and flee or abandon your vehicle, as your plate numbers are linked to your SSN. So if the police stop you on the highway for a traffic offence, they actually find out who you are once they punch your Driver's License number into their car's computer, which is networked to their database.

Now since the tragedy of September 11, 2001 there has been unprecedented collaboration of State police and FBI activities. So if you leave Texas, to go and reside in Maryland, within a certain time you have to change your Texas Driver's license to a Maryland one. As your Texas DL was tied to your SSN, the Maryland one is also tied to your SSN, so all the information the police in Texas possessed about you becomes instantly available to the police in Maryland. Some people don't like this and feel this is a sign of the Orwellian state, but they do not know what it is like to live in a country where you can be completely anonymous.

Beyond law enforcement, the SSN helps business and commerce. It helps with issuing credit to consumers by banks and merchants and is the backbone of a consumer credit rating system. The way the credit system works is each merchant or company consults your records at the Credit Reporting Agency, using your SSN, before they allow you to make a purchase on credit. These agencies keep records like your date of birth, previous addresses, etc, which they get each time you apply for a credit purchase. They also possess records of credit you had applied for in the last 3 to 7 years, those which were approved, records of your faithfulness in making your monthly payments (merchants report your payment records to the agencies monthly), and records of any other merchants who have made a credit inquiry about you. These records are available to any merchant who wants them, and they are also available to law enforcement agencies. The Credit Agency report gives merchants an idea of how credit-worthy you are (how much you owe against how much you earn), and helps them determine whether your application for credit should be approved.

Apart from when you actually apply for credit, merchants also make generic inquiries about credit-worthy consumers. Based on what your credit standing is, they offer you credit for their products if they deem you to be a good consumer.

This means Company A could sell you a car on credit,

company B could sell you a house on credit, company C could sell you electronics on credit, etc, while you agree to pay each of them a certain sum every month (including principal and interest) until each loan is completely paid off. Each of these companies get paid by the bank backing the credit sale, so, in essence, you are taking out a bank loan for the purchase. What links all these transactions to you is your SSN, which is the first thing they ask for when you apply for a credit purchase.

In America, people buy homes for as little as 3% of the cost, spreading the balance over a 30-year period. The banks are able to back these home purchases because buyers are identifiable and traceable through the system. There is no anonymity.

So what about the rental business? Car rental businesses are able to flourish because the rental companies are able to trace renters through the system. If you rent a car, they will process your ID, which is usually your State-issued Driver's License. Some renter companies demand your social security number, which they need to process your rental application. Some will not rent to you if your credit score is not considered strong enough, based on the assumption that someone with poor credit rating is a rental risk. But if you have good credit, you could walk into a car rental place and drive out in 15 minutes with the car of your choice. The rental business is only possible because renters can be uniquely identified in the system.

So the credit system helps boost sales far beyond what it would have been if there was no credit system. It leads into boosting the Gross Domestic Product of the American economy.

With what I have seen in America, any nation that does not implement a unique, mandatory National Identification numbering system is hugely short-changing itself, its people, and its economy. For it to be beneficial, such a system must be the foundation of commerce, with an independent credit reporting system built on it. Strictly enforced legislation should be put in place to ensure that the system is not corrupted by criminals and cheats.

While the SSN has been very useful in making things work in America, I often wonder if this number has anything to do with a number (or number system) spoken of in the Bible in Revelations 13 verse 17:

"and that no one may buy or sell except one who has the mark or the name of the beast, or the number of his name."

This was where the Bible spoke of the number of the Anti-Christ. The only similarity here is the phrase "no one may buy or sell except one who has the mark... or the number." In the American economy, generally speaking, you cannot buy, sell or rent many things; neither can you do much else if you do not have a SSN. So, I really wonder...

Taxation and Tax Revenue

Taxes bring huge revenue to the government, and the revenue helps fund government projects and activities. The huge tax revenues mean the government has more resources to make the lives of their citizens better. When Americans talk of tax-payers' money, they really mean it. This is different from my native country, where less than 10% of income-earners pay taxes and millions evade and avoid taxes. The regulatory regime back home is, at best, weak, but certainly corrupt. So when people in my native country talk of "tax-payers" money, we might need to verify if the speaker himself is actually a tax-payer, or if he had paid the correct taxes.

In America, you can safely say that fear of the Internal Revenue Service (IRS) is the beginning of wisdom. Everyone working in America is required, by law, to declare their incomes and taxes to the IRS by April 15 of each year. It is a crime to present false returns to the IRS. The IRS examines the returns and may decide to ask more questions.

If, by the guidelines of IRS, you have paid more taxes in the previous year than you should, they give you a refund, usually within 3 weeks of you filing your tax returns. If, on the other hand, you had underpaid taxes, the IRS demands payment. You cannot owe the IRS and get away with it. The IRS has powers to seize and sell your property, garnish your salary, freeze your bank accounts, and take over anything you own in order to get payment.

If you fail to file your tax returns, the IRS could take you to court, which could send you to jail, regardless of who you are in society.

Americans pay their taxes because they see where the money is going. They see the roads (which get repaired quickly and a facelift every few years), the police (which keep them safe in and out of their homes), the prowess of the military (which deters foreign aggressors), the school system (which gives their children good education at low costs), the food and agriculture inspectors and regulators (whose work gives the rest of the society a necessary peace of mind in making purchases), and so on. The use of taxes is visible in the daily lives of every American.

You don't see government agents and touts chasing people for tax evasion and tax avoidance. People paid. While it may be argued people pay taxes because the tax laws are strong, it is my opinion that two things make people pay their taxes in America.

One reason, as we have mentioned, is people see where the tax dollars are being used: road maintenance, caring for special needs citizens, law enforcement, schools, and many social services programs.

The second reason is that particular examples continue to be made of people who don't pay and get caught, or people who don't pay enough, especially the rich and famous. The popular actor Wesley Snipes was sentenced to prison recently for tax evasion, for example. So because the law and its enforcement is effective, and continue to show examples, nobody needs to chase people in order to get them to pay their taxes. As you have till April 15 every year to file your tax returns, only fools mess up the date.

Law Enforcement

One of the most important reasons why things work in the USA is law enforcement. Law enforcement works and America is a relatively safe country to live in. The country is safe not because everyone is allowed to carry guns, but rather because the law enforcement is very functional. The police are well-trained, well-equipped, educated, and know their job. Don't get me wrong, we do have some corrupt people among the police, and there are racists among them.

But all in all, the police are efficient. In most parts of America, you don't need to install burglar-proof bars on your windows. You may not lock your front door, yet no one will come near your home.

A typical police officer carries on him enough equipment needed to subdue a small crowd. They have communication equipment which works at remote locations. The police may not be your friend, but they show they are your protectors.

In the American Federal system of government, I believe that true federalism is practiced. There are different layers of government, Federal, State and County, each with a mandate to protect the citizens. Each layer has its own police, the town or city police, the county (or local government) police, and the state police. Everyone knows their limit and jurisdiction issues do not arise, or they are well-managed when they do arise. Such issues are not visible to the populace.

While there is no police organization at the Federal level, there is the Federal Bureau of Investigation (FBI). The FBI operates nationwide. Because each state is independent of the other, jurisdiction issues arise when crime and criminals cross state boundaries. New Jersey police, for example, have no jurisdiction to investigate or prosecute a crime in neighboring Pennsylvania. The FBI coordinates investigations across state boundaries. It is largely non-uniformed, and their presence is not as visible as the uniformed police. But believe me, they are there, probably checking you out for one reason or the other.

The reason most people don't speed and get into road accidents is because there is the ubiquitous police presence. Many times, the police go in unmarked vehicles, and the vehicle you may be trying to overtake at break-neck speed may be that of police officer driving in an unmarked vehicle because of speed racers like you. If the police, in marked or unmarked vehicles, stopping you and issuing you a ticket is all there is to it, it would have been okay.

When the police car starts flashing its light behind you, you are required to pull over to the side of the road and stop. You DO NOT get out of your car, but wait in your car until the police officer comes to speak with you. It would be useful if you keep your hands on the steering wheel so the officer knows you are not hiding a weapon. But the officer doesn't come to your vehicle immediately. It takes him an eternity to come and speak with you while he takes his time to find out more about the owner of the vehicle, by punching the vehicle's plate number into his computer. When he has the information he's looking for, and having taught you Lesson Number 1 in patience, he gets out of his car to come and speak with you.

He would likely ask for the car registration and your own driver's license. He would most likely discuss with you why he stopped you, and with the two documents, he walks back to his car to do more research on you. It takes him another eternity to return to you, thereby teaching you Lesson Number 2 in patience.

If in all his inquiries, he finds any anomaly or criminal activity, he may radio for backup, and escalate the issue. Otherwise, he may give you a ticket, a warning or just engage in a chat and drive off.

Now, if the speed limit was 65 mph, and going at 75 or 80 mph could bring you all this delay, wouldn't you rather go at 65, rather than spend the next 30 minutes at the road side, bypassed by all the vehicles you had sped past?

The Watchdogs - Regulatory Organizations in America

While many Americans take the work of regulatory organizations for granted, these unsung, under-appreciated institutions which regulate products and services in America are responsible for the good quality of life in America. These organizations ensure the quality of the eggs on your breakfast table, the safety of your child's toy, the cost of the electricity you use, and the quality of the water that flows out of your faucet.

For example, there is the Department of Licensing and Measures, which regulates the gasoline pumps. They make sure that when you pay for 10 gallons of gas, you actually get 10 gallons. If this organization doesn't work, those pumps could be manipulated, wrongly calibrated, and you might get only 4 of the 10 gallons of gas you bought delivered into your tank, even if the pump reads 10 gallons. The next time you go to get gas, look at the pump. You will see a marker which shows the last test done by the Licensing and Measures Department. I have lived in places where, sometimes, the pumps are manipulated and you only get air and a little gas pumped into your tank, while you still pay for a full tank.

Then there is the Federal Trade Commission, which ensures fairness of business organizations. There is the Federal Communications Commission (FCC), which ensures the quality of broadcasts on radio and TV and doesn't allow pornography or offensive media to flood our homes. There is the US Department of Agriculture, which monitors the quality and safety of the food you buy. There is the FDA, which tests and monitors drugs and medicines. There are also many other organizations, some of them faceless, which monitor and regulate the quality of air and pollution, the strength of bridges, the meter in your taxi-cab, the safety of the vehicles on the roads, the quality of imported goods, etc.

These governmental organizations are actually what make the standard of life in America high. If they didn't do their jobs, or if they cut corners, America would not have the respect it has in the world today. The world wants to drive American cars because of the safety features, eat American food without thinking twice, and use American medicine because they are sure of what they are taking.

The world respects America, not for the number of nuclear weapons it has, nor the size of its fighting armies, but because of the stringent maintenance of quality standards in every facet of human life. These regulatory organizations, which neither carry guns nor drive tanks, are responsible for this, but I am not sure if Americans themselves realize or appreciate it. You see, you don't value something if you always have it and never risk losing it. I should know.

Chapter 13

What Makes America Great

So because the government is afraid
of the people, governments initiate and
effect policies which make the lives of
the people better.

13
What Makes America Great

The People

The most important factor for the greatness of America are the American people. Every one of the political parties, Republican and Democrat, works hard to please the people. The reason they do this is because the American Constitution and the application of it has in-built mechanisms by which any government can be removed. The principal vehicle to remove an unpopular government is elections, and all politicians work hard so that, by the next election, they are not jettisoned for another set of leaders. The competition for elective offices is often fierce, and the party in opposition is always quick to point out the failures of those in power.

Another way an unpopular government can be removed is by impeachment, which is usually initiated by the legislative arm of government. Impeachments are controversial, especially when the political party controlling the Executive branch of government is not the one controlling the Legislature.

There is also the Recall vote, which is like an impeachment, but initiated by the people, when a group is able to get a certain number of voters sign a paper saying they no longer want the elected leader to continue in office. This can also be controversial, as political parties can surreptitiously engineer their members to initiate the process.

So because the government is afraid of the people, governments initiate and effect policies which make the lives of the people better. The elected leaders at the Federal level are afraid of the people and, in order to please them, formulate policies and execute programs that benefit the people. At the State, County and Township levels, the same thing happens. The end result is that several projects and policies which better the lives of ordinary Americans get done.

But leaders don't wait until the next election cycle to know what the people think, only to be surprised at the ballot box. They also conduct public opinion polls where they ask people what they feel about a policy or project of government. If they find the public does not understand their policies, they take to the streets and educate the public so the public perception of the policy or project becomes favorable. Alternatively, they reverse course and decide not to pursue the project or policy.

In essence, the people, through the power they possess at the ballot box, indirectly rule the country and get the projects and policies they want. This truly makes it the government of the people, by the people, and for the people.

If you grow up in a third world country and start experiencing all these things after you started living in America, you wonder why the same could not work back home. But then, you remember that, back in your country, elections seldom seem to matter. Those in power appoint the officials who conduct the elections, who, in turn, dance to the tunes of those who appointed them. So when elections are held:

i.   the results are falsified, or

ii.   more voters than those registered get to vote, or

iii.   ballot boxes get stuffed beforehand with fake votes, or

iv.   ballot boxes vanish in transit, or

v.   voters are intimidated, or

vi.   electoral officials are intimidated.

When they get into power, the "elected" official does not feel accountable to the people, because, in reality, they did not elect him in the first place. He sees the money and resources of the government as an extension of what he owns, and because he has access to such huge resources and controls law enforcement, he has the ability to manipulate, buy off, or terrorize political opponents. To make it even worse, the opposition is often weak and insincere. They are often looking for a way to get rid of the current cheats and oppressors so they themselves can become the new cheats and oppressors. This is often the public perception, so, in essence, the public does not trust the opposition or see them as saviors. They only root for the opposition when the excesses of the current rulers are no longer bearable, not because they really believe voting the opposition in will truly bring the fruits of democracy.

This is how people can live their entire lives without ever seeing true democracy at work. There is nothing as good as democracy, but, in many countries of the world, what is called democracy is just not real. I have seen both sides!

The Rule of Law

Everyone in America has respect for the law, rich and poor alike. Everyone expects equal treatment before the law, regardless of their stations in life. States make and enforce laws of their own, separate from Federal laws, but neither state nor federal laws are allowed to target any particular individual or group. The watchdog institutions, the courts, press, legislature and executive branches will ensure such laws don't stand. This is best seen where different parties control the executive and the legislature. For example, if the state legislature makes a law meant to oppress or target some political group, the governor will veto the law.

If the state executive and legislature are from the same political party, and the governor assents to the bill, making it law, the federal attorney general can take the state to court if someone's rights are violated by the law. The press usually joins in the fights, putting pressure on the State executive and legislature. This is evident from a recent case, where Arizona made a law requiring police officers to demand immigration papers when they stop a person, even for routine traffic check. Arizona borders Mexico, a source of illegal immigration, and the executive and legislature are controlled by the Republicans. Some people in the state say undocumented immigrants from across the border have messed up the job market, as they are willing and able to work for pittance, far below the minimum wage. The state government passed the law to address the situation, aiming to make the state unlivable for undocumented immigrants. The press got involved. Civil liberties organizations got involved. The Federal Department of Justice sued Arizona, claiming the law would violate the rights of some citizens. In June 2012, the U.S. Supreme Court ruled on the case, upholding the provision requiring immigration status checks during law enforcement stops, but striking down three other provisions as violations of the US Constitution.

Here's the bottom line: in America, no one arm of government can target a person or group without getting a fight on its hands. So before a law is made or executive action is taken, those involved would have weighed it carefully, probably asking: for all the noise that will follow, is it worth it?

Caring For Human Life and Human Dignity

America cares for the life of the average American. Since the system knows everyone, people don't just die without record.

My wife's earliest job was as a Therapeutic Support Specialist. She was working with a special need child in his school to help him understand what was being taught. This is one good thing about America. Every American life is valued as important enough for the government to provide special care when it is needed.

On my commute to work in New Jersey, I see a road sign declaring, "Deaf Child." This meant a deaf child lives in the neighborhood, and, therefore, motorists should drive with extra care. Can you imagine? One deaf child in a neighborhood made the road sign necessary! If you were the parent of that child, would anyone need to plead with you to pay your taxes?

In developing countries, many disabled people are on their own, and they have no other option but to go around begging. Mentally handicapped people roam the streets and are beaten and abused by people. Those in government-run mental institutions are poorly treated and given little food, while the money meant for their food and care goes into corrupt pockets.

The reason you don't find many mentally disabled people roaming the streets of America is not because they don't exist, but are in group homes, being cared for by private organizations and agencies paid for by the government. These agencies are funded and closely monitored by the Social Services Department. There are people with disabilities from very young ages to very old ages. If you are physically hand-icapped and unable to work, you receive stipends from the government while your handicap persists, even if it is for the rest of your life. This is the price society gladly pays for those with disabilities, recognizing that they too have a right to life, a right to liberty and a right to the pursuit of happiness.

The Checks and Balances of Government

The founding fathers of America put in place the 3-tier system of government which America practices today. Each tier is independent from the other, each one serving as a safeguard against the other. The most visible is the Executive arm of government, where the day-to-day work of setting and executing policies and programs get done. The legislature also exists at the Federal and State levels, to make laws that govern how and what the Executive does. The Judiciary is the Father of the house, to settle quarrels between the Executive and the Legislature, as well as quarrels the citizens have with these two tiers of government.

Somehow it has worked.

In recent years, however, serious politics has entered the system. Republicans oppose a policy not based on merit or common sense, but because it was a Democrat who proposed it, and Democrats oppose a policy just because it is a Republican idea. There is no middle of the road, and the word "compromise" is now a euphemism for weakness. The result is that everything is now politics, and politics is everything. You would think that those who have served years or decades in Congress would rein in the younger, hot-blooded ones who need to prove that "I-am-also-there-doing-something," but you find these older ones are not arbiters but protagonists. They start trouble now more than they did in their younger years. There is no father-figure in the US Congress, no sage, no wise old man or woman who everyone defers to. Everyone behaves as if it's a house full of little kids, with each one trying to shout loud enough to drown out the others.

I would expect a person like Republican Senator John McCain, who has nothing to prove to anyone, earned the hearts and the minds of every American, and whose political career has been so sterling, to be a father-figure of the US congress. I would also expect that someone like Democratic Congressman John Lewis, who was an active young man in the Rev Martin Luther King's movement and who has earned his "stripes," to have also become a father-figure in US politics. They should be the kind of people any sitting President should have a conference with before enunciating a major policy. But where we find Senator McCain or Congressman Lewis today is far beneath them and I hope they will rise to their deserved levels, regardless of which Party occupies the Oval office.

I also find it odd that Supreme Court justices don't always rise above partisan ideologies, and in some cases have delivered judgments based on Republican versus Democratic party ideologies. Those appointed by Republican Presidents tend to vote together, and those appointed by Democratic Presidents tend to vote together. The only logical explanation I have is, while they are not expected to be active politicians, these justices were Republicans or Democrats before they became Supreme Court justices, and are simply expressing their inner convictions when they give partisan judgments. But should this be so? Shouldn't they be seeing themselves as accountable to more than 300 million people, rather than to the political parties they affiliated with, or even themselves? This was what the Chief Justice John Roberts did recently when he sided with the Democrat-appointed justices to uphold the Affordable Care Act (aka Obamacare). All other justices stood along party lines.

Sue Me, I Sue You - the Law of Tort

Another thing that makes America great is the law of tort, which, as I understand it, makes people (and organizations) liable for their actions and inactions. The individuals or companies which brought injury to someone are held responsible for their actions. The courts might fine them or ask them to pay monetary damages to the injured party, or both.

People sue other people, companies, governments, and agents of government. Friends sue friends. Relatives sue each other. Neighbors sue each other, etc. There was a case of two cousins driving in the city who had an accident. The passenger cousin sued the driving cousin for negligence! Of course, the tab was picked up by the insurance company.

Until I got to America, I didn't know you could quantify "pain" and "suffering." In America, this is a whole field of business, spearheaded by lawyers and aided by victims. Lawyers actually advertise openly, seeking people who have been injured. They promise to get "large settlements" for their clients. Truly, there are many cases where, due to negligence, greed and the carefree attitude of some service providers, you really need to sue for poor or negligent services, but many people exploit the system for money. The question is: with what meter do you gauge the pain someone says he has suffered? Or how do you measure anguish, or emotional disturbance?

One snowy December morning, I was going to work. There was a steep descent to the main road from the apartment complex where we lived. When you descended the slope, you had to look out for vehicles coming from either direction, before you turned onto the main road. The vehicle in front of me had hit the one in front of it as that one was waiting for the road in front of it to clear. As I was descending the slope, I struggled to control my car and eventually slightly hit the car in front of me, making it a 3-car pile-up. While we were assessing damage on our cars, a fourth car came behind me and hit me, also slightly. Now there came a fifth vehicle down the slope. It was a man who was driving, presumably with his wife by his side. He avoided the fourth car, stayed to the right of all of us, and was gently slowing down on our right as it approached the main road. Somehow, as it neared the main road, it veered a little to the left and gently, as gently as it could, it slightly touched Car Number One. Before we could say Schwarzenegger, the man had called 911, the emergency services. Fire trucks, ambulances, and police vehicles raced to the scene. The woman was carried from her car on a stretcher to an ambulance, which whisked her away. All of us who had hit each other earlier were just looking at each other. You see, before this couple arrived on the scene, some of us had fallen several times while trying to inspect our cars for damage. I was sure I had fallen 3 times and, on one occasion, I had hit my head. We briskly stood up each time and continued what we were doing. Yet this woman, who was uninjured, called an ambulance. Since the ambulance carried her off the scene, she would then claim injury and sue the insurance company of the other driver to get a "settlement."

People like this woman abuse the system, making the cost of health insurance higher for the rest of society.

The law of tort makes it possible to sue a manufacturer, retailer or service provider when poor service is provided. Your dry cleaner would do their best not to mess up the clothes you brought in because they could be sued. Your fast food company will make sure every aspect of their service is above board to avoid lawsuits. In order to avoid people making claims of negligence or poor service, they spend a lot of money to train their employees on customer service. But people still abuse the system.

There was a woman who went to McDonald's to buy coffee on her way to work. She claimed the coffee was too hot and scalded her hand. She got a good lawyer and got a settlement of millions of dollars. While I don't get it, someone told me the woman was rightfully awarded. There was a man in DC who sued a dry cleaner for over $7 million dollars. There was outrage from a lot of people and the press over this abuse of the system. How expensive was the clothing that you're suing for over $7 million? The judge dismissed the suit.

You see, whenever we heard incredible stories of how Americans con the system, the con men always seemed too audacious and we Nigerian immigrants say to ourselves: They say there is 4-1-9(four-one-nine) in Nigeria, what Americans do is 4-1-10. (Section 4.1.9 of the old Nigeria criminal code made advance fee fraud a crime, but today, all fraudulent practices are generally termed 4-1-9).

We say this, not to justify fraudulent practices, but to say that in the crime business, the numero uno con men and crime originators are in advanced countries like the USA. If you don't believe me, check out a program called "American Greed: Scams, Scoundrels and Scandals" on CNBC. This program presents several well-researched and well-documented cases of brazen, unbelievable, audacious criminals and fraudsters who make the 4-1-9 criminals of Nigeria look like kindergarten students next to University professors.

The law of tort is useful, however. It makes people take responsibility for their actions and non-actions. If it snows and you fail to shovel the snow in front of your house and someone passing by falls or is injured, you could be liable for a lawsuit. So, in order to save yourself from a lawsuit, you come out after it snows to shovel the snow in front of your homes, and, of course, so you, too, will be able to drive in and out.

The Pride of Labor

It does not matter where an American works, or what he does, he is proud of the work he is doing and the contribution he is making to the organization. He takes his works seriously, fulfils the hours he has committed to, and takes charge. The store attendant says to you: "I don't have it in blue, but I can get the blue in for you by Tuesday." He speaks as if he owns the company and as if he controls the entire supply chain; yet he might be on a salary of just 12 dollars an hour. The reason he is able to do this is because, at every point along the line, he takes pride in what he is doing. He does not see himself as one little guy, but as the representative of the company at that point. So in most places you go, workers take ownership and responsibility.

The salesperson also does this to ensure the company does well and he is able to keep his job. He has to keep the job because, if he gets fired, he would have a problem taking care of his family and his financial responsibilities. And in America, everyone is on his own; nobody looks out for anybody as you would in Africa, where if you were out of work you could still depend on your parents, uncles, siblings, and other relatives for months. You live in their homes, you ate their food, and you even take money from them for your expenses. This does not exist in America.

The American worker is also aware of his rights and knows he could sue his employers if treated badly in the workplace. If the worker is a member of a union, he could, at the request of the union, join a picket line to protest against the policies of the company, without fear of retaliation. The laws governing the actions of employers and employees are well enforced, no matter who owns the company.

More importantly, no company likes to have bad press. If the press descends on a company for wrongful practices, consumers could shift en masse to an alternative product, which means loss of customers, loss of revenue, loss of face, loss of competitive stand, and possibly the loss of the company.

The United States Postal Service (USPS)

More than any other organization, I believe that the United States Postal Service (USPS) has contributed greatly to the economic development of America. Letters are delivered to your home and office every day, except on holidays. If you mail something in any part of America, it will be delivered in any other part in a day or two. Whatever you put in the mail is safe; no one will open your letter or steal its contents. Americans take this for granted, but it is only because they have not seen the other side.

You see, the marvel about the USPS is that it is a governmental institution, yet it works with the precision of a private company. All over the world, government institutions are derided as inefficient. The picture that comes to mind is that of an elephant at the starting line of a 100 meters dash. When the race starts, it takes it too long to even begin to move, and every step after that is laborious. But the USPS runs a countrywide service that works everywhere and every day, even in winter. It recruits labor, pays its staff, and, according to its advertisement, is self-sufficient.

I come from a country where the postal system does not work, so people don't use the post office. Letters people posted were being dumped into the bush. Mail was opened and the contents stolen. If you needed to send someone an important document, you used a private courier, never the post office.

Here, you could put a million dollar check in the mail, and it would get to its destination. What makes the postal system work is that laws have been made (and enforced) that make it a crime to tamper with letters. Also, the post office competes with private courier companies like FedEx and UPS, and doesn't want to lose grounds to them. It is also a crime for anyone to tamper with your private mailbox. Advertisers and people marketing their services cannot open your letter box in front of your home to put in advertising materials. There is also a law that says no one apart from you, none at all, has a right to open a piece of mail addressed to you. Recently my daughter, who is in law school, picked the mail from the mailbox. There was a letter from her school, which was from the financial aid office. She had spoken to me a couple of days earlier about an issue with her financial aid. I reached for the letter, and as I was opening it, she reminded me, "Dad, you know it is a felony to open a letter not addressed to you!" Of course, you know what the African father in me would say, something like: "what do you mean, weren't you the one who brought the issue to me?" Well, thankfully, no one got sued, and no one was prosecuted. But the laws safeguarding the postal system in America are serious!

The Entrepreneurial Spirit

There is a profound entrepreneurial spirit in America that continually drives the economy. People fabricate anything and sell anything and the idea marketplace is flourishing. With the advent of computer technology, people are thinking of how to inject one computer device or the other into your work and life, and make some money by providing you solutions that you never knew could be devised.

The great thing about introducing new products in America is that if the product is useful, the large population of the country guarantees you a huge and ready market. Even a not-so-useful product will still get a few people who would want to give it a try, and one try from many people is all the entrepreneur needs to be able to get enough resources to make the product better.

Back in my home country, there is a strong entrepreneurial spirit too, but the difference I have seen in America is that people combine ideas, resources and strength more than they do in Africa. In Africa, business organizations tend to be one-man operations, which, if successful, will then employ people to work for the business owner. What I've seen in America is people are not always after sole proprietorship. Here you see friends combine ideas and resources, classmates combine ideas and resources, brothers combine ideas and resources, and so on. People are not really looking to take credit for an idea, but they feel okay just to be part of something that works.

This, I believe, is the strength of American businesses. Because it is not just one person formulating the ideas, doing research, and sourcing markets for the product, businesses tend to be more successful.

One thing I also seen in America is when a business does not succeed, or is struggling, the owner(s) sell it or shut it down without being seen as failures. People buy into businesses and sell off businesses without qualms. There is no loyalty.

This is radically different from what I grew up knowing in Africa. If you started a business, which, as I have said, is often a one-man business, and the business fails, it is directly seen by everyone (including your friends and family) as your personal failure. Of course it has to be, because it s your personal business. You created it, funded it, ran it, and if it failed, you caused it to fail. As a result of this perception, people keep pumping money and resources into an idea that refuses to take off. If you see any African business that is struggling, or is not a great idea, but the owner keeps putting money into it, it is because the business failure would be seen as personal failure.

You see, in the agrarian African life we grew out of, everyone had his own farm and everyone worked hard at it. Only the farm of the lazy and indolent would not succeed. It was often overgrown with weeds, because in his laziness he did not weed or prune. So if you heard of someone's farm failing, (except for a natural disaster that affected other people too) it was seen as the result of laziness. This idea is what flowed into African business, which makes it almost an abomination to fold up a failing business.

In 1999, about 10 months after our arrival in Philadelphia, I started a computer training school in Philadelphia all by myself. A computer training school business was a good business at that time because knowledge of home computers was just beginning to spread, and jobs requiring computer skills were opening right and left. Due to my job, (to which our H1B visas were tied) the only time I had to run the school was in the evenings after work. I was the marketer, the instructor, and the entrepreneur. I was able to recruit someone to man the office and answer enquiries, but then, the rent and staff salary was predicated on my own salary from my job. I couldn't take a bank loan to fund the business because I had very little credit.

The business was hampered by the fact that I had no partners, and with the knowledge of sole proprietorship I had brought from Africa, I didn't think of seeking a partner or investors. So, while the idea was great, the business failed and I shut it down after two years. If I could do it again, I would do it the American way: invite partners and investors who are interested in the business. This would share the risk, spread the workload, and give the business more of a chance to succeed. As someone told me, it is much better to own 1% of General Motors, than 100% of Me-And-My-Sons Inc.

Many new immigrants have caught on to the entrepreneurial spirit of America, and many are no longer contented with having a good job and staying there for years. Immigrants are now opening businesses and buying franchises.

We have a number of people who go to auctions to buy used vehicles and ship them to Africa. Because people use their vehicles carefully in America, avoiding accidents in order to keep their insurance costs down, after several years, those vehicles still look new. So when these vehicles are sold off here in order to acquire newer models, many are often snapped by Africans who ship them home for resale of for the use of some relatives. There, they are put to several additional years of use.

Many African doctors end up owning their own practices, sharing costs with other doctors.

What has not caught on is the joint ownership of businesses. Perhaps as people gain more confidence, this will be another trend that settling immigrants will imbibe and adopt.

Chapter 14

America is not Heaven, Americans are not Saints

So when people in Africa and other parts of the world struggle to get a visa to America, with the hope of making it to this "heaven" at last, little do they know of what lies ahead. Heaven certainly does not share borders with Canada and Mexico.

14
America is not Heaven, Americans are not Saints

America is not heaven

Before they come to America, many view America as a place of happiness, joy, and plenty. The way they see it is similar to what God described to the Israelites before they entered the Promised Land:

> "For the LORD your God is bringing you into a good land, a land of brooks of water, of fountains and springs, that flow out of valleys and hills; a land of wheat and barley, of vines and fig trees and pomegranates, a land of olive oil and honey; a land in which you will eat bread without scarcity, in which you will lack nothing; a land whose stones are iron and out of whose hills you can dig copper." (Deuteronomy 8:7-9 NKJV)

To an extent and in general terms, this probably describes the United States of America. Food is not expensive, and the land is beautiful, and diverse. Oh America is beautiful, and a lot of care is taken to preserve its beauty. From coast to coast, all levels of government work hard to make the cities and the suburbs beautiful. Within the same country, you have vast deserts, mountain ranges, huge rivers, oceans and bays over several time zones.

There are opportunities here. You face no restrictions just because you came in as an immigrant. You can buy and own property if you have the money. You can start businesses and compete with the "sons of the soil." You have the freedom to practice your religious beliefs, and to build your church, mosque, synagogue, or temple. The only thing required of you is that you play by the rules. Everyone is required to play by the rules and the law is often applied equally to everybody.

America offers everyone the ability to have a decent job, earn a decent income, live in safety in a decent home or apartment, and meet one's basic financial obligations. America also offers freedom: freedom of speech and expression, freedom to form any association (as long as it is not aiming to destabilize the country or harm others), and freedom to contest elections. Everyone has a right to pursue their dreams and live in any part of the country they desire without fear.

With God on your side, with hard work, you can rise to become anything in America. This is what is called the American Dream. The American Dream is a nationally accepted idea that everyone should have the opportunity to prosper and succeed and rise to higher stations in life regardless of background, origin, sex, or skin color. The idea is copiously espoused by all Presidents and other leaders, and greatly encourages immigrants like me.

In all of these, America surpasses most nations of the world. It is a very tolerant society. Even in my native country, you cannot contest for elections in certain areas if you are not from there. In some parts, your property can be vandalized or your family killed if you are of a different religious belief than the people around you. So in truth and deed, America is light years ahead of many nations in this respect.

However, despite the fact that America is like the Promised Land, it is not heaven. You have to work very hard here. People work till they are very old. You cannot afford to lose your job, and if you do lose it, you have to scramble to get another one before your unemployment insurance runs out (if you even had some). You cannot afford not to have income because you have to pay your bills.

The bills are payments for all the services and utilities you use. You have to pay, unfailingly every month for:

- rent or mortgage bill,

- cellular phone bill,

- landline phone bill (if any),

- electricity bill,

- water bill

- waste disposal bill,

- heating or gas bill,

- cable or satellite TV service bill

- college loan bill (if any),

This is not an exhaustive list. It could be very much longer, depending on your circumstances.

You cannot avoid them. You've got to pay your bills, otherwise your services will be disconnected. This is not a country where you give the meter reader a bribe so they falsify the figures and it is certainly not a place where you can bribe the people who disconnect your services. In fact, most of the services are disconnected right from the control center of the service provider.

Also, in America, most people cannot afford to hire any help. You drive yourself, you clean your own home, you mow your own lawn, etc. It is a do-it-yourself nation, at least for most people. Back in my native country, a young college graduate who is working is able to employ house-help to do household chores. There, a young couple is able to employ a live-in nanny as soon as they start having children. Most families in Nigeria are able to recruit a chauffeur, and if you have a yard to be mowed, there is plenty of cheap help who would be grateful for the opportunity to render service at a pittance.

Most of these helps in Africa do not earn anything close to the minimum wage. Hired help must be paid minimum wage in the USA, so most people help themselves. Some African people who brought house-help to America and were paying them under-the-table wages were caught, charged in court for exploitation and sentenced to fines and prison time. If the law in America says something is the minimum wage, then it is the least you can pay any staffer you recruit. This is why most people in America don't recruit house-helps, because most people are not that rich.

Unless you win the lottery or take a bank loan, you don't normally come into big money that suddenly changes your lifestyle drastically. In my native country, if your relative, friend or classmate gets an important position, he could give you a contract with wide margins and you could become rich for life! This cannot happen in America. Things are done more transparently and more competitively.

In America, most people (especially in Caucasian communities), are not their brother's keepers. Everyone is expected to fend for himself. Your problem is your problem and not anyone else's. However, this is not common in immigrant African and Hispanic communities. You are more likely to see a white or African-American homeless person than a homeless immigrant African or Hispanic person. It is not that some people are worse than others; it is just a difference in the value and belief systems.

My niece, who was living in Philadelphia, hosted me on my arrival in America. At that time, she, her husband, and their two little kids were just settling down. The only job she was able to get was Tech Support in a company in Baltimore, MD. The job didn't pay much, but it was better than nothing. She drove to Baltimore two to three times a week, staying with friends on days she couldn't drive back to Philly. Things were not easy then, but they managed. Whenever she heard people talk of Nigerians struggling to get visas to come to America, she would say: "Oh, why is the US Embassy wasting time? Give them visas! Give them visas and let them come and see how easy America is!" She was talking from experience, as she herself was struggling through the system at the time. Living in America could be hard, if you are not properly situated.

So when people in Africa and other parts of the world struggle to get a visa to America, with the hope of making it to this "heaven" at last, little do they know of what lies ahead. Heaven certainly does not share borders with Canada and Mexico.

Americans are not saints

Americans are not saints; they are as human as every other nationality in the world.

When hurricane Katrina struck New Orleans, the government response was terrible. Help did not arrive on time and many died in the aftermath of the disaster. When people ran out of food and basic necessities, they resorted to looting shops and grocery stores. When there was another hurricane in New York and power was cut and people's lives were disorganized, people looted grocery stores and shops.

When there was a huge power outage affecting most of North-East US, and most of New York was covered in darkness, people had to walk several miles to get home, as the subway system was paralyzed. On that occasion, people also looted stores and shops under the cover of darkness. In all these situations, law enforcement was too overwhelmed to stop them.

These are exceptional situations, but they drive home the point. When a human being is deprived and has no other means to survive, he will resort to chaos and anarchy. Resorting to anarchy is not the preserve of one race or country alone. It is a normal and expected human reaction to one's environment. Where there are catastrophic circumstances, chronic lack of or insufficient basic resources, the animal in man comes to the fore. The struggle for those resources is often the struggle for life.

But apart from uncommon situations like hurricane Katrina, there are rarely situations where people have to struggle to buy things or encounter chaos in everyday living.

As has been noted elsewhere in this book, tricksters and fraudsters exist in many places in America. The truth is not always plain, and what is plain is not always the truth. You have to decipher every word in an advertisement to know the truth. One single word alone could be what the advertiser is hiding under in making dubious claims, and you always have to read the fine print.

There are fraudsters and cheats, 4-1-9ers and 4-1-10ers. From time to time we hear of serial killers, and of psychopaths who kidnap women and lock them up for years. There are cities that experience multiple murders a day, and in many large cities, there are people who would mug you for just five dollars. Some neighborhoods in America are worse than the worst crime neighborhoods in my native country. Incidents of mass shootings happen almost every month in one part of the country or the other, and homelessness exists in most large cities.

I have listed these to show, though America is a powerful, rich and prosperous country, problems also exist in America, as they do elsewhere. The rich also cry.

Recognizing this, however, does not reduce the greatness of this country. It does not take anything from the goodness of the heart of most American people and it does not diminish the meticulous efforts by successive administrations to make this country one of the greatest and most peaceful nations on earth.

What this shows is just that there is no perfect human

system and there is no man-made system that does not have shortcomings.

Yet, America is our home and is truly great, and promises greatness in the future.

It is the land of the free, and the home of the brave.

CPSIA information can be obtained
at www.ICGtesting.com
Printed in the USA
FFOW05n1118131114